life rules

For further information:

The Kabbalah Centre
155 E. 48th St., New York, NY 10017
1062 S. Robertson Blvd., Los Angeles, CA 90035

1.800.Kabbalah www.kabbalah.com

First Edition
April 2005
Printed in USA
ISBN 1-57189-299-0

Design: Hyun Min Lee

life rules

how kabbalah can turn your life
from a problem into a solution

yehuda berg

www.kabbalah.com™

dedication:

To my mom. You taught me the wisdom of Kabbalah every day by being who you are—by your pure and unconditional love of people, the Creator, and of life; by your unwavering certainty that there is a gift in all that comes your way; and by the completeness with which you experience the adventure of every moment. You shine like a beacon of Light for all of us, giving strength amidst any storm. Now you are touching so many more people. Congratulations on your new book, *God Wears Lipstick*. I love you.

acknowledgments:

I would like to thank the many people who have made this book possible.

First and foremost, Rav and Karen Berg, my parents and teachers. I will be forever thankful for your continual guidance, wisdom, and unconditional support. I am just one of the many whom you have touched with your love and wisdom.

Michael Berg, my brother, for your constant support and friendship, and for your vision and strength. Your presence in my life inspires me to become the best that I can be.

My wife, Michal, for your love and commitment; for your silent power; for your beauty, clarity, and uncomplicated ways. You are the strong foundation that gives me the security to soar.

David, Moshe, Channa, and Yakov, the precious gifts in my life who remind me every day how much there is to be done to ensure that tomorrow will be better than today.

Billy Phillips, one of my closest friends, for your help in making this book possible. The contribution you make to The Kabbalah Centre every day and in so many ways is appreciated far more than you could possibly know.

To Jane Ratcliffe, thank you for helping me to find the words that have been locked away inside me since my youth. My hope is that by sharing my experiences with the gift of kabbalah, it will empower those who need it most.

To Hyun Lee, Christian Witkin, and Esther Sibilia, whose contributions made the physical quality and integrity of everything we do live up to the spiritual heritage of this incredible wisdom that has been passed on to me by my father, Rav Berg.

I want to thank Rich Freese, Eric Kettunen, and all the team at PGW for their vision and support. Your proactive efficiency gives us the confidence to produce more and more books on Kabbalah so that the world can benefit from this amazing wisdom.

To all the Chevre at The Kabbalah Centres worldwide—the evenings we share together in study fuel my passion to bring the power of Kabbalah to the world. You are a part of me and my family no matter where you might be.

To the students who study Kabbalah all over the world—your desire to learn, to improve your lives, and to share with the world is an inspiration. The miracles I hear from you every day make everything I do worthwhile.

In the process of writing this book, I sent a rough draft to a friend of mine asking her for feedback. I wanted to share what she wrote:

Dear Yehuda,

Firstly, I want to tell you how important I think a Teenage Kabbalah book is to bring into the world at this time. I don't think I said that to you when we met. The story I am about to share with you just reinforced the importance for such a book.

By no strange coincidence I went to pick up my 16 year old daughter from a party the other night and while waiting for her in the car an acquaintance of hers, a lovely 16 year old girl named Molly, whom I had only met several times before, knocked on my car window and asked tearfully if she could talk to me. Of course, I invited her to sit in the passenger seat. She was very upset and emotional. She came to me, she said, because she saw how close I am to my daughter, Jordan and she felt she could confide in me. Of course I told her that while my daughter and I are close, we have our share of issues too but I was glad to be a sounding board. I asked her what was troubling her. Her story was not unlike so many teenagers—her parents didn't understand her and she felt hatred toward her overly untrusting and critical mother. She spoke of how she wanted to run away and how unhappy she was at home. She was in therapy as was her mother but nothing was getting better. We sat and talked for well over a half and hour. I found myself sharing my still limited, but powerful Kabbalah teachings with her. I told her that she had the power within herself to start living proactively and could begin making changes at home herself. I told her that she was not a victim nor the prisoner of miserable teenage years and that she could have light and happiness in her life now, not later. We spoke together at length about how she needed to pause and not react to her mother's rageful outbursts. She hugged me at the end of the half hour and left my car in a much better place. Three days later a woman with whom I had never spoken before called me on my cell phone. (I had given Molly my cell and office number if she wanted to ever talk again)

"You don't know me," the stranger on the phone said, "My name is Sharon. I wanted to call and let you know . . . Whatever you said to my daughter, Molly . . ." she chocked and stumbled on her words . . . "Thank you."

Yehuda, I have waited in my car for my daughter to come out of parties many times in the past. Never has a teenager knocked on my window to ask for my help. I had just finished reading your manuscript a few days prior. For me, it was a powerful message of just how needed Kabbalah is for teenagers everywhere.

Warmly,
Linzi

introduction:

surviving life

intro

ongratulations! You are holding in your hands a book that contains the power to change your life, to change the lives of your friends and family, to change the lives of everyone everywhere. Sometimes these changes will be fun, and at other times they will be extremely challenging. But if you carefully follow each of the 13 steps that lie ahead, your life will begin to feel the way you always dreamed it would.

As you know, things are not always what they seem at first. Your best friend last year may not seem like such a great person this year, and that teacher who seemed so mean on the first day of school may have turned out to be your favorite. One illusion in life that gets us into lots of trouble is the feeling that there isn't enough good stuff to go around. It's like watching your favorite dessert being sliced before your eyes and everyone reaching in for a big, thick piece, and it's still nowhere near your turn. You start thinking you're going to be left out, so you quickly come up with strategies to make sure you definitely get your share. Most of your thoughts involve keeping someone else from getting theirs. Now imagine the relief you'd feel if your mom walked out of the kitchen carrying two more trays of dessert—fresh out of the oven—and announced that there were several more baking. You'd realize then that there was more than enough for every-body. And you'd realize that there was no need to expend all that energy on stressing over your slice—the size of it, the qual-ity, the order in which you received it. You could have relaxed and just enjoyed yourself the whole time.

I was lucky. My mother understood the notion that the good things that really matter have no limits. I could fill this book and several more with stories of the kindness she showed not just to my brother and me, but to everyone we met. My father and mother were studying a form of ancient wisdom called Kabbalah at a time when few people even knew what it was. Because of this, our family was considered eccentric, to say the least. We had few friends and little money, but honestly, our hearts were always full. During my high school years I attended a yeshiva, or Hebrew school. Most of the kids there weren't fond of me. I was often ridiculed for my parents' unusual beliefs. In fact, I was asked to leave before my final year—all this just because my father was teaching the wisdom of Kabbalah! Yet the same kids who would torment or ignore me loved my mother. When she dropped me off at school in the morning or picked me up at night, kids would run over to say hello and would offer to carry whatever she might have been holding.

I believe this is because my mother's love and compassion is boundless. I remember one time my teammates and I were headed to an "away" basketball game, and our van broke down in the middle of a snowstorm. I called my mother, and she and a friend turned up, squeezed us all into two cars, and whisked us off to the game. We weren't even late! None of my teammates was surprised that my mother had bailed us out. She could be counted on, and they loved her for that.

Another time, a ninth grader was hit by a car outside of school. The accident wasn't severe, and the boy wasn't a friend of mine (he wasn't even in my grade). Nevertheless, my mother, who happened to be waiting to pick us up, scooped him into her car along with my brother and me and dashed to the hospital. We all waited there while he received stitches, and then my mother drove him home. When it turned out that he lived with his guardian in a dilapidated apartment, my mom hired two people to clean and fix up their home. Bear in mind that we had very little money ourselves. Often dinner for us was just rice and beans. But somehow my mom managed to care for others and still make sure we ate well and were clothed appropriately. Her dessert tray was unlimited.

When a boy from my school was diagnosed with Hodgkin's disease, my mother sent hot meals over to his house and arranged for volunteers to help care for him. His parents were very grateful, and she and the boy formed a close bond. In fact, when he passed away, it was on her birthday.

My mother never stopped to wonder what she might be giving up by helping someone, or how her life might be diminished if she worked to improve another's. However, this level of love and compassion is not easy to achieve. My mother and father had been studying Kabbalah (the basis for this book) for many, many years by that time. My mother had been diligently working on the very steps you are about to learn. But bear in mind—and this is important—that before we can truly help others, we must first learn to help ourselves. It's like the oxygen masks on an airplane. We are instructed to put on our own oxygen mask before assisting small children or others in need. The reason for this is that if you don't know how to help yourself—and are therefore not fully functioning—you will not be able to help anyone else. Without your own oxygen mask in place, you may pass out before safely securing someone else's. Then, clearly, you will have been of no help at all!

The wisdom contained in this book is very old—older than any of the major religions practiced today. Tracing back more than 4,000 years, it began with Abraham, who is recognized as the father of Judaism, Christianity, and Islam. Abraham wrote a book called *The Book of Formation* which recognizes that there are two spheres affecting our lives: spiritual and physical. Much of our time is spent in the physical; it is here that we make demands on ourselves for nice clothes, cool friends, and perhaps even experimentation with sex, alcohol, and drugs. But this is not our only realm. By opening our mind to the spiritual alternative, we allow a transformation to occur, after which we begin to realize that acquiring something in the material world fulfills us for only a limited time.

Abraham's wisdom was passed down to Moses and then to Plato and Aristotle. Countless scientists, including Sir Isaac

Newton, were students of Kabbalah—not to mention psychiatrist Carl Jung and the seminal playwright William Shakespeare. Yet throughout this time, the teachings of Kabbalah were kept secret.

Fast-forward to the 20th century, when Rav Yehuda Ashlag deciphered these profound texts, making them accessible to you and me. Without Rav Ashlag, we would still be stuck watching the good things in life circulate right under our noses without knowing how easy it was to get our share. Rav Ashlag passed the teachings down to Rav Yehuda Brandwein, who then passed them down to my father. Each generation suffered greatly for disseminating these teachings. Rav Ashlag was badly beaten and left to die in a pool of his own blood. My father was barely able to support his young family. But now there is a flourishing new generation of teachers who are dedicated to making Kabbalah accessible to everyone. Without them, you wouldn't be reading this book at this moment. You'd be out on the streets with friends or sitting at home playing video games or downloading something you're probably not supposed to. Not that pleasures within the physical realm are "bad." It's just that they pale in comparison to the pleasures of the spiritual realm.

Originally only great scholars were allowed access to kabbalistic books and teachings. This is because Kabbalah teaches that The Bible is actually encoded—that the words and stories contained within its pages, although valuable in themselves, also contain another, more potent layer of meaning. Many feared that if this wisdom fell into the wrong hands, it might be abused. Even in the absence of malicious intentions, it was thought that a student who was unprepared for such potency might be overwhelmed, as if you were being handed the keys to a race car when you've never even driven around the block. But modern scholars have discovered that given the proper education and support, Kabbalah can be understood even by the layperson. That's why it's important that you move through this book slowly, considering each step carefully. There's no rush. Kabbalah has existed for countless decades. Its power will still be there when you reach the final page.

The great thing about Kabbalah is that it's not intended for just one particular ethnic group or religious contingent. It's meant for you, exactly where you are in your life right now. Whatever you have overcome in your life and whatever difficulties may lie ahead, this is the perfect time to be reading this book. There are no gimmicks. You don't have to practice these steps on a remote mountaintop or deep within a cave—although you can feel free to do either, provided that someone knows where you are! You don't have to do anything weird at all in order for this stuff to work. The work takes place within your heart and soul, so you can practice it while eating breakfast, in a line at the video store, in the middle of a math test, or even during an argument with your best friend.

You have probably struggled at one point or another to make sense of your life. While often painful, this struggle is good! It means you are instinctively looking inward, searching for greater meaning. Kabbalah can help you understand the purpose of your life, the purpose of pain and suffering, and the choices we can make to find peace and fulfillment not only for ourselves but for others.

First, a key word: Light. This is the never-ending joy my mother had let into her life. This is unconditional love and compassion. It existed long before any of us; it's where we all came from and where we are all headed. We've all experienced it briefly. Any moments in which you have felt genuinely happy, when joy has flooded through you—that's the Light. When you are pleased by a job well done, when you are tingling from falling in love, when you are perfectly relaxed on a boat on the ocean, when you are laughing so hard with friends that you think you're going to explode, when you watch someone you love earn something they deserve—the source of all of this is the Light. It feels absolutely amazing, right? Wouldn't it be nice if life could feel like that all the time? Well, it can. But there are rules.

Consider the light bulb in your ceiling. You flip a switch, and on it goes. But the light bulb is not the source of the light; the real source is an electric generator somewhere you can't even see. And there are rules around how much light can be emitted as well as when and why. The same is true with the Light of Kabbalah.

One of the common mistakes we all make is to confuse a person or thing with the Light. For instance, nothing feels as good as falling in love. So naturally we associate our girlfriend or boyfriend with those happy feelings and assume that person is the source of them. But it doesn't work that way. No other person can guarantee us the good feelings of love we are after. It's the way we act in relation to other people that brings the Light. And that's what this book is all about.

The Light is what animates us, what fills us with joy and abundance and generosity. It's home. Every time you open your heart, mind, and soul to the Light, you're closer to home.

Think of this book as your well-lighted path.

don't believe a word you read.
test-drive the lessons learned.

1

1

life rules

chapter one: don't believe a word you read, test-drive the lessons learned.

M y junior high and high school years were often rough. My yeshiva classmates were just like me, except for the fact that they weren't. Or, more precisely, I wasn't like them. They were being raised in traditional Jewish families and were attending religious school because it was what they were supposed to do. But most of them didn't want to be there. They had more interest in playing together after classes let out than in anything our teachers had to say. They returned to school the next morning only because their parents made them.

Most of my classmates made fun of me. They called me names, and they teased me. Yet as odd as it may sound, I wanted to go to school. My parents never made me. In fact, they never made me do anything. Which isn't to say that my brother and I could sit around reading comic books and eating candy bars all day. Quite the contrary, we had a very disciplined life. But by educating us in Kabbalah, my parents allowed us to be active participants in our own decision-making process. Taking responsibility for my own choices turned out to be a life-altering decision, and one that I will discuss further in the following chapters.

Before we go on, let me take a minute to talk about religion and spirituality. These words are often used interchangeably, but they're not the same thing. Religion usually embraces some sort of metaphysical or supernatural belief and includes lots of dogma and ritual. You're expected to accept its theories as realities. It's like being in school where all the cool kids are wearing a certain brand of jeans, so you think you should be wearing them as well. The theory is that without these jeans, you will never fit in or find happiness. And if you run out and buy a pair (which most of us have done at one point or another), that's blind faith.

My father never let me get away with blind faith. He encouraged me to take responsibility for everything in my life. When I demanded "the" jeans, he pointed out that there were other

life rules

chapter one: don't believe a word you read. test-drive the lessons learned.

brands available—or corduroys, for that matter, or cargo pants. I could even wear a skirt if I wanted to! My father wasn't seriously suggesting that I show up to class in a skirt, but he was pointing out that I did have choices. He was challenging me to consider what I really wanted to wear—and why. This process of getting to know yourself better—of getting to understand how you tick, and learning how to reshape your desires into proactive, beneficial behavior-is what spirituality is all about. Frying an egg can be spiritual if you bring the right mind-set to it.

When I was 14 or 15 years old, I decided I didn't want to belong to the "in crowd" anymore. I looked at my peers—even the most popular ones—and their faces looked empty. None of them seemed genuinely happy. Sure, they had all the right clothes. Some of them were driven to school in fancy cars. Some had girls from other schools handing them their phone numbers on tiny ripped corners of pink paper. But none of this seemed to be bringing them satisfaction or peace of mind. And none of their parents seemed content, either. They were all fine people, even those who were cruel to me, but they didn't have what I knew was possible.

I saw my first glimpse of the Light in my parents. They faced incredibly harsh times but were never without a smile, a kind word, a helping hand, and even a joke. I was 14 when my father began schooling my brother and me in Kabbalah. We would begin our study after dinner and would often go well into the night. (This is how I became a night owl, which I remain to this day.)

I remember making a conscious decision that I would apply myself to the steps laid out in Kabbalah—the ones I've included here. The jeans, the Nike sneakers, the latest video games-it wasn't bad to want these things, or even to have them. But to rely on them was not going to take me where I wanted to be.

life rules

chapter one: don't believe a word you read. test-drive the lessons learned.

Before I learned Kabbalah, I had been studying traditional Judaism at my yeshiva. Maybe some of you have done so too—or perhaps you embarked on Christian studies or attended a Catholic school. In class, I had been taught to believe whatever was written in The Bible. This is true of many religious—and academic—teachings. As students, we are rarely asked to test-drive other people's ideas for ourselves. This is dangerous business. For instance, if you were to come across something on the Internet that said, "A flock of sheep flew over Jamaica today," would you believe it? Probably not, because you have seen sheep, and you know with certainty that sheep can't fly. But if you didn't have firsthand knowledge, you might take this article as truth. Recently we've seen a rash of scandals at prestigious magazines and newspapers involving reporters who have lied to the public, duping even their editors. Television shows have been sued for telling lies. And radio stations are often making on-air corrections concerning previous broadcasts. But if you miss the corrections, miss the headline that a reporter lied, or miss the lawsuit, you will continue to believe the original error.

We have been raised to believe that much of what we read, see, or hear in the media must be true simply because it's being presented as such. Did you know that when Orson Welles' production of *The War of the Worlds*—a play about aliens attacking the earth—was aired on national radio in 1938, people who had tuned in late thought the broadcast was real? Panic swept the country, causing traffic jams, clogging telephones lines, and interrupting public services. People actually believed we were being attacked by aliens simply because they had heard it on one radio station. We must be more careful about what we choose to believe—and what we choose to reject. Otherwise we may think our lives are in danger when in fact we are only being entertained. Or vice versa.

The same holds true for religion. At heart, all of the major religions adhere to the same basic belief: Love thy neighbor as

life rules

chapter one: don't believe a word you read. test-drive the lessons learned.

thyself. Only the methods vary. Unfortunately, many religions impose lots of rules and regulations on their followers. And they don't allow us the freedom to figure out if their teachings even make sense. If you do things because you're supposed to— whether they're religion—based, parent-based, or peer-based- you will never find happiness. You'll never meet up with the Light. Blind faith is what we are trying to combat with this book. Questioning everything is an excellent place to begin. So is wel- coming spirituality into your life.

I had friends in high school who didn't want to live according to the principles and rules of their parents or teachers. I'm sure these adults meant well, but unless my friends decided for them- selves what path made sense, they weren't going to get very far. If your parents tell you not to touch a hot oven, it is quite differ- ent from actually touching that oven, however fleetingly, and learning firsthand just why you don't want to do that again. If your friend tells you that snowboarding feels like flying through heaven, that's merely a nice theory or belief until you yourself are out on the slopes. In the interim, you can choose to believe your friend, withhold judgment, or not believe your friend at all. After all, another friend may have broken a snowboard and told you that the sport is hell. Don't be afraid to collect information and form your own opinions. That's why we are here—to be informa- tion hunters so that we can gain certainty. Belief leaves room for doubt. Certainty doesn't.

This is not to say that we need to wear ourselves out with test drives. Your parents may warn you about the hot stove, and they may turn out to be telling the truth. Later on they may warn you not to drink water while lying flat on your back because you may choke, and this also turns out to be true. Over the years, enough of a track record may be established that by the time they warn you about the dangers of drugs and of drinking and driving, you can trust their insight without testing it because they've proven themselves to be reliable. It is my hope that you will find another such reliable source in the teachings of Kabbalah.

Sometimes you're not sure what to believe when you first hear something new. This is normal. Try listening to your gut. You will know that the wisdom is pure if you find yourself saying, "Wow, I already knew this—deep inside I always felt this to be true." If you don't have this feeling—if something you've heard or read or seen doesn't turn out to be true to your experience—throw it out. This is true of all wisdom, including this book.

○ You can't find lasting happiness if you do things simply because someone else told you to do them; nor can you find that happiness if you believe in something because someone else told you to believe in it.

○ What we want is the Light. Certainty—through exploration—is one of the tools with which to achieve this.

○ Religion and spirituality are not the same thing. The former is often rigid and preachy; the latter is a life path.

I recommend that you keep a journal as you read this book. At the end of each chapter you will find a set of exercises. As you finish a chapter, you can complete the exercises in your journal as well as do some free writing about your response to the chapter. What thoughts were stirred in you? Were there points you passionately agreed with? Make note of these. How about points that you didn't understand or even disagreed with? Start a fresh page and make note of these too. See if these points become clearer as you make your way through the book. You have 12 more steps to go, so give yourself time to absorb and process this information. Scholars have spent lifetimes delving into this material, so don't expect to grasp it all overnight. Profound change requires patience. Be kind to yourself, and move at your own pace.

Take some time now to think about everything you just read. You might want to discuss this chapter with a trusted friend or relative. If you do, however, pay careful attention to where your thoughts end and theirs begin.

Consider your purpose on the planet. Why are you here? Be specific. Make a list. And be honest. This book will serve you only if you are truthful with yourself. Describe how you came about your basic beliefs. How many came from careful consideration and have been regularly road tested? How many are on the list because someone else told you they were true? There is no right or wrong here. You are simply learning how to observe your mind. And even if every single belief comes from outside yourself, no worries. This is the perfect place to start, because if every belief were already your own, you wouldn't have as much material to work with!

chapter two:

there are two basic realities: our 1% world of darkness and the 99% realm of light!

2

2

ike Veruca Salt in *Willy Wonka & the Chocolate Factory*, we seem to go through life shouting, "I want it now!" But remember what happened to young Veruca when she finally got her hands' on a golden egg? She fell down the chute for bad eggs, her indulgent daddy tumbling helplessly after her. Granted, Veruca is an extreme example, but we all know that when our desire calls, its voice is loud and clear. Certainly some of us have taught ourselves patience, and others among us have learned the value of quality over quantity—but still our wants never seem to be satisfied. This is most apparent when it comes to our basic comfort zone. When we're cold we put on a sweater, and then soon enough we're too warm. So we take the sweater off and get a cold drink. Then, of course, we're cold again, only now we also have to use the bathroom. And so on. We are sated, but only momentarily. Similarly, we want the "right" stereo. And after enough fuss, we get it. Then we might feel satisfied for a few days, but before long we notice there is something else we want: the "right" speakers or the "right" CD player. Or maybe we need to be listening to the "right" band.

We're just as restless with friends and family. We decide that knowing this or that person will make us cool. But after we get to know him or her, we're not any cooler than before; inside we're still the same, and we don't feel any better about ourselves. That dark hole of desire isn't one smidgen smaller. In fact, our new friend might make us even more aware of things we don't have. This sort of desire is painful because it never stops. It's insatiable. It's the desire for external gratification. And it belongs in what is called the 1% Realm.

A realm is a self-contained world. If any of you are writers, it's what you create when you scribble down a story. Its characters, their homes, their jobs, their family and friends, and their pets all live within the realm of your tale. The same holds true for a painting or a photograph—whatever you decide to paint or shoot belongs in that realm. Movie directors create realms every day.

life rules

chapter two: there are two basic realities: our 1% world of darkness and the 99% realm of light!

The 1% Realm is what most of us are familiar with, although most likely we're not aware of it. We have spent most of our lives in it, as have the majority of our friends and family. It's the physical realm, the realm of the emotions and of the five senses. Here people and objects are solid and touchable. They have smells and tastes specific to them. The body is our lifeline in this realm and needs to be cared for properly. Time and space call the shots here. We are born, we grow up, we grow old, and then we die. A brand-new car eventually breaks down and cannot be repaired, so it gathers rust until its solid-metal body is shot through with holes. Everything in the 1% Realm comes to an end. Here, nothing is infinite. There is no possibility of infinite happiness or infinite joy, not to mention infinite life.

This is also the realm of reaction, and of the chaos that ensues because we react to most things without thinking. If there's one thing I hope you take away from this book, it's the need to take a moment to think, think, think before reacting to a situation. The purpose of this book is to teach you to make conscious, informed decisions—decisions made from certainty, not from mere belief; and decisions that reveal the Light. We'll discuss reactive behavior more thoroughly in Chapter Four, but until then, experiment with pausing—even if it's just for a deep breath— before you react to any circumstance that upsets you.

Granted, there is a lot of pleasure to be had in this realm of ours—going to the movies, dancing, family vacations, sexual exploration, staying up all night with friends, getting a new car, getting your first job. But as we've discussed, this feeling comes and goes. That's the nature of pleasure. Try to think of an example of pleasure that has lasted in its original, pure form. You may think, "Well, I felt pure love for my kitten!" Yes, but didn't your kitten grow into a cat and lose some of that cuteness you once loved about him? And doesn't he use the kitty litter daily, or sometimes twice a day—litter that you are now in charge of cleaning out? And doesn't he want your undivided attention,

life rules

chapter two: there are two basic realities: our 1% world of darkness and the 99% realm of light!

often when you need attention yourself? Naturally, he is still bringing you heaps of happiness, but it's not uninterrupted. It's not Endless.

This is another key word: Endless. It too is from whence we all came. It's what we call the 99% Realm. It's where the Light is. If the 1% Realm is the realm of pleasure, then the 99% Realm is the realm of fulfillment. We get there not by satisfying our external needs, but by turning our attention inward. In the 1% Realm, we work ourselves into a lather trying to scratch itches that never stay in one place—itches that are insatiable because they are only symptoms. In the 99% Realm, we can begin to address the cause.

Consider when you have a cold. One day your throat hurts, the next day your eyes itch, the next day you're running a temperature, and on the final day your nose is stuffy. Each day you have a new symptom to tackle and a new remedy with which to tackle it. This is not bad. In fact, at this point it is necessary; symptoms do need to be addressed. But the cause of these symptoms is a compromised immune system. So if we treat only the symptoms, they may fade, but chances are good that they will surface again fairly quickly—most likely with greater power. Rather than showing up as a cold, they may now manifest as strep throat or pneumonia or even cancer. So if we turn our attention only to alleviating symptoms, nothing is truly changing. If, however, we treat the cause in addition to treating the symptoms, the next cold will likely be less severe, as will the one after that. More time will pass between colds. And eventually we may stop getting sick altogether.

When I was in high school, my parents bought matching dress coats for my brother and me. As I've mentioned, we didn't have much money, but we needed decent outer clothing to fend off the harsh New York winters. My parents liked these new coats. They liked the fact that they matched. They thought we looked

life rules

chapter two: there are two basic realities: our 1% world of darkness and the 99% realm of light!

handsome in them. But my brother and I hated them. The kids at our school were wearing hooded parkas and Mets jackets. No one—and I mean no one—was showing up at school in the kind of wool three-quarter-length coat that one might wear to a funeral. This made our already low standing in the school even worse.

I will never forget the first moment I saw that coat. I had been waiting what seemed like forever for it, and I had high hopes for what it was going to do for me. But when I saw it hanging there, I almost cried. Of course this was my 1% speaking—the part of me that believed something external could fix my life. But eventually I came to have deep appreciation for that coat. My parents had worked very hard in order to be able to afford it, and they had selected it with great care and love. When they looked at me in it, they felt fulfilled. As I came to understand this, I developed a profound affection for my ugly coat. I no longer worried about what other kids might say. Part of me had touched the 99% Realm.

The time before I developed this appreciation, however, was rough for me. I felt guilty and unworthy. But my father had begun teaching me about Kabbalah, and some of it was sinking in. During my struggle with the coat, I focused on the step you are reading about now—the realization that two realms exist simultaneously. I realized that by putting so much energy into being embarrassed by my coat, I was wasting energy that could be channeled into the 99% Realm. And at that point, I made a conscious decision to redirect that energy somewhere more productive. For me, this was the beginning of tapping into the 99% Realm—the beginning of opening myself to the Light.

The Light denotes unending happiness and constant joy—not just regular happiness and joy, but *unending* happiness and *constant* joy. Stop for a moment and consider what this might feel like. It's the difference between pleasure (which, as we've already established, comes and goes) and fulfillment. We desire the unlimited. We don't want to do well in our classes half the semester. We'd rather not date someone we just kind of like. We don't want to be friends with someone for just a month and then have to start all over again with someone new. Or be on the baseball team for just half the season. We'd rather not have our mother stop doing drugs for only half the year. We want our desires to be constantly understood and continuously fulfilled. This is what happens in the 99% Realm.

Before you start getting upset that you don't have the 99% Realm *now*, let me suggest that you actually do. We all have access to it, but for most of us it's fleeting. Think of the moment you put the final touches on a project that you fiercely believed in—one that took lots of time and effort to complete. That rush of a job well done is the Light. Or how about that time you shared your already-too-small bedroom with your friend because her father was beating her, and her life was made easier because of your kindness? That too is the Light. Marveling at a perfect row of tulips. Singing "Happy Birthday" to your kid brother. Turning down drugs offered by particularly persuasive friends. Receiving well-earned praise from a teacher. These are all aspects of the Light. So you *have* touched the Light. The trick now is figuring out how to get it when you want it—and how to make it last.

Have you ever had a gut feeling that if you went to this one particular party, even though you were tired and grumpy, something good was going to happen to you—and when you did, you met your future best friend, or fell in love, or just had a great time? Or have you ever just known that if you walked down a certain street, something bad would happen, and you later found out there was a drive-by shooting on that street in which a boy was killed? This is your intuition guiding you. And your intuition is provided by the Light.

According to Kabbalah, there is a curtain separating the 1% Realm from the 99% Realm. This curtain is all that keeps us from

life rules

chapter two: there are two basic realities: our 1% world of darkness and the 99% realm of light!

total fulfillment. Intuition is one means of pulling aside the curtain, but there are others. This book will familiarize you with the curtain. And with each step you take, you will draw it open further.

One important thing to remember is that desire is what draws us together. Desire for world peace or desire for war. Desire for pizza or desire for a salad. No matter how profound or trivial, human desires are our common link. Everyone desires happiness; no one desires suffering. Yet we often mistake someone else's search for happiness—their avoidance of suffering—as being "anti-me." How often, for example, have you thought a friend, a teacher, or a relative was mad at you because they'd been giving you less attention than usual, only to discover they'd had a personal tragedy in their lives—perhaps a death, an illness, or a family quarrel—that was simply making them withdraw for a bit? Not just from you, but from everyone, until they felt settled again.

I once knew a young woman we'll call Anna who ran into the sister of her first great love (we'll call him Matt) on a boat trip. The two women chatted for a while, and then Anna gave her number to Matt's sister, who said she would happily pass it along. Anna was incredibly excited at the prospect of hearing from Matt. He had meant a lot to her both during their relationship and over a number of years, but then they had lost touch. She remembered their times together sweetly and considered herself very, very lucky that he had been her first love.

For the first few days after Anna got home from her boat trip, she skipped across the room to answer the phone every time it rang. But it was never Matt. Weeks passed, and then several months. Anna took Matt's not calling personally. *I must not have mattered as much to him as he did to me, she thought. If he had truly had feelings for me, then he would have called me by now.* Anna's thoughts became worse and worse until finally she became quite depressed about the whole thing.

Several months after that, Matt called. He and Anna had a lovely conversation, at the end of which he apologized for not having called her sooner. "I've had a horrible skin disease," he confided in her. "And I wanted it to clear up before seeing you."

When we take the actions of other people personally, this is our ego speaking, telling us that we are the center of the universe— that everything that happens in our lives revolves around us. Our ego is the curtain separating us from the 99% Realm. The more we can tame it, the further the curtain will draw open.

How often have you heard or used the word *suddenly*? Suddenly my big brother ended up in jail; suddenly she broke up with him; suddenly the coach kicked him off the team; suddenly my mom moved out. But how sudden *is* sudden? For instance, have you ever woken up to suddenly find a new tree in your backyard? Or to find that your hair had suddenly grown ten inches? Or that you suddenly lived in a new home? Not likely. "Sudden" implies a sense of chaos, a sense that things happen to us, rather than the deeper truth that we happen to ourselves.

Happening to ourselves is a good thing. In fact, it's a great thing! It's about the best thing that could happen to us! No one else is calling the shots. And while this introduces a whole lot of responsibility for our thoughts, words, and actions, it also allows limitless possibilities. We have already, perhaps unwittingly, shaped our past. And we have the power to shape our present and our future as well. As you read this book, keep this thought in mind: If something happens to me, I am locked in the 1% Realm. I am reacting. But if *I* am happening to me—good or bad—I am connecting with the 99% Realm. I am being proactive. Don't expect to understand this completely now. This idea is a huge gold mine that we will continue to explore in the pages that lie ahead.

life rules

chapter two: there are two basic realities: our 1% world of darkness and the 99% realm of light!

Most of you are probably familiar with chaos theory, or what's sometimes called the "butterfly effect." A butterfly flapping its tiny wings in Tokyo can trigger a change in atmospheric pressure that eventually creates a tornado over Iowa. A woman slamming down her bedroom window in London on a dreary winter's night can set off what will become a cloud formation on the sunny beaches of Brazil. Everything is connected. Weather appears random to meteorologists only because they are unable to perceive and measure all the millions of influences that contribute to it—such as flapping wings and shutting windows. In fact, however, there is an order that is hidden from our eyes.

This also holds true for our lives. No matter how chaotic our lives may seem, everything that is happening has a specific cause. But just as we do when we have a cold, we experience primarily the effects. We are largely unable to see true causes because they're tucked behind the curtain. But remember, the curtain is our ego. It belongs to us. And therefore we can change it.

There was a time, before you were born, when people didn't make the connection between the dumping of toxic waste in the ocean and thousands of people becoming seriously ill from eating ocean fish. It seemed as if a plague had hit. It was scary. People felt as if something awful was suddenly happening to them—something over which they had no control. Eventually, through careful research and investigation, the connections between the toxic dumping, the fish, and the illnesses were made. Cleanup efforts began, and people stopped getting sick. Chaos is the misperception that there are no connections. In fact, everything is connected. Everything.

Interdependence means that your presence on this planet matters. Just like the gentle flapping of the butterfly's wings, your actions resonate beyond your wildest dreams. Therefore, act responsibly. And don't sell yourself short. Also remember that your neighbor's actions are resonating as well. So don't sell your neighbor short, either.

In closing this chapter, let me say that there is nothing wrong with wanting new jeans or wanting to kiss the cute girl in your class or wanting to pass your driver's test. Having your desires satisfied in this realm is part of the natural process of living and learning. Kabbalah doesn't ask you to give up all earthly pleasures. You don't have to shave your head or live in a monastery. The 1% Realm exists. The pleasures of this realm are indeed pleasurable. But the important thing to remember is that they don't last. And they cannot be counted on to transform your mind so that you can get to the realm in which they do last. So think of them as rest stops along your greater path—places to hang out and get a little rest and relaxation. The underlying desire is the one to pay attention to: our desire for the Light.

○　Desire is our driving force.

○　Two realms exist simultaneously: the 1% Realm where we spend
most of our time, which cannot
ever satisfy our true desires, and
the 99% Realm, which provides
endless joy and happiness.

○　Everything is connected.
Because of this, nothing "suddenly" happens. There is always a
cause. Chaos stems from ignorance of the interdependent nature
of all things.

○　Symptoms or effects should be
addressed, but in order to make
lasting change, you must go to the
root, or the cause.

Everyone wants happiness; no one wants suffering. Be careful not to mistake another's search for happiness as a threat to your own.

Our ego is the "curtain" that separates the two realms from one another. Only by removing the curtain can we access the Light.

Endlessness is the home of the Light.

External desires are not "bad," but they will not deliver the Light, no matter how many we receive.

Appreciation is an important tool in revealing the Light.

Turn to a fresh page in your journal, and make a list of your desires. Put down everything that comes to mind no matter how small or how foolish it may seem. You might want to be able to go skiing with your best friend and his family this weekend. Or perhaps you want your sister to stop doing drugs. You might want your parents to stop fighting, or your teacher to stop calling on you so much in class. You might want to grow up to be a famous athlete. Or to end world hunger. Or to save people's lives. Or to make so much money that your parents never have to work again. Perhaps you want that cool shirt you saw online. Or the CD you heard at your friend's house. Or you want to be able to sleep more calmly, or to stop worrying so much, or to lose five pounds without having to throw up all the time. Or to gain ten pounds of solid muscle. Just put that desire down on paper.

When you've done that, write next to each desire how you think you might feel if you attained it. How might your life change? Now consider what stands between you and attaining your desires. Why don't you have these things now? As always, there's no right and wrong here; you're simply trying to gain some insight into what you desire from life. Without knowing your true desires, you don't stand much of a chance of attaining them! So be honest. Keep your notebook in a private place, and know that no one is going to read this but you!

chapter three:

everything that we truly desire from life is spiritual light!

3

3

When I was young, my father used to tell me a tradition-al kabbalistic tale about a kingdom in which all any-one ever did was complain. One man complained he that didn't have sufficient milk to feed his family while his neigh-bor had enough for his wife and daughter to bathe in. Another man complained that his job required him to work 12 hours a day while the fellow down the street had to work only nine. A woman complained that her own child cried through the night, not allowing her to sleep, while her sister's child never uttered a peep. The people complained so much that eventually the King ordered everyone to gather in the center square, and to bring with them a pencil and paper.

Grumbling, the townspeople assembled. Those who had arrived early sat on the few stone benches that were available, while the latecomers stood and glared at them enviously. It took the King several attempts to quiet his unhappy kingdom, so preoccupied were his subjects with all their complaining. When the King final-ly had everyone's attention, he instructed each person to fold his or her paper in two. On the right side, they were to make an honest list of everything they had, and on the left an equally hon-est list of all the things they didn't have.

There was a great rustling of paper, followed by murmurs and craning heads as people compared lengths of lists—but after some time passed, the chore was complete. The King now instructed his subjects to go from person to person in search of a list that they found more appealing than their own. When they found one, they would be free to take it. But you must take it all, he explained—the good and the bad. There was then a chaotic rush toward the wealthiest man in the kingdom. His lands and herds were vast, and his imposing home was staffed by count-less servants. But a look at his list revealed that his son was dying of an incurable disease, and his wife didn't love him any-more. Not even the poorest person in the kingdom wanted a loveless marriage and a dying child. So the crowd rushed on to

life rules

chapter three: everything that we truly desire from life is spiritual light!

the next wealthiest man. But while his lands, too, were vast, he was unable to enjoy their abundance because of the bitterness he carried in his heart over the rape of his daughter. The father of the kingdom's next wealthiest man had gone mad and required constant care. The next wealthiest after that had lost his leg in an accident, and the next suffered from terrible depression.

And so it went, until every person in the small kingdom had compared lists with every other. The sun had set. No one had eaten. No one had gone home or fed the animals. Finally, the King strode majestically to the center of the square and asked how people felt about their lot in life now. Slowly the people nodded, as though waking from a long sleep.

Not one list had been exchanged.

Thanks to the wisdom of their King, these townspeople had swept aside the curtain of their egos and made contact with the Light. What a potent moment they had all shared! They returned home with a sparkling new appreciation of their lives. But it is easy enough to imagine that in a day or so—or certainly after several weeks—these same townspeople might have forgotten everything they had learned on that day. It's easy to see them once more coming to envy the neighbor who was able to sleep late, or the ones who had servants to wash their clothes and fluff their pillows. This is because we are not able to access the 99% Realm whenever we choose.

But imagine if we could!

As we have learned, here in the 1% Realm we are dealing with the effects, but in the 99% Realm we are able to access the cause. Cause is the key to our spiritual transformation. Remember the persistent cold we discussed earlier? If we keep treating the itchy throat, the runny nose, or the clogged chest, we will certainly enjoy some relief, but chances are good that the cold will come back with even greater force before long. But if we do some investigation and discover, perhaps, that we are allergic to dairy products, then we will have found the cause! By focusing on our diet, we can then get rid of our symptoms for good. Think of it this way: If you alter a branch of a tree, you change the branch. Modify a leaf, and you change the leaf. But if you can manipulate the genetic information inside the original seed, you can affect the entire tree—branches, leaves, fruit, everything.

Staying with this analogy for a moment, think of the 99% Realm as the DNA of our reality. It is the seed. The root. The cause of all causes. This is why the exercises contained in this book are useful: They will help you identify your symptoms and guide you to their causes. Once you have identified a cause, you can begin to work with it. Otherwise, life will continue to feel as if it is happening to you.

If we set aside our material desires in life—those desires that are connected with the 1% Realm—we find that the desires we share cannot be measured or weighed on a scale or held in our hands. We can't wear them to school or drive them to pick up a hot date. We can't lose sleep over whether we will pass them or not. Nor can we sell them for extra spending money. We certainly can't smoke, drink, or snort them. Our nonmaterial list might include items such as peace of mind, physical safety, financial security, happiness, health, love, contentment, personal fulfillment, relief from fear and anxiety, freedom, control, and wisdom.

These are all qualities of the Light.

Although my high school years were painful in many ways, I never felt empty. This was because I always knew I had the love of my parents and my brother. This certainly wasn't something cool I could wear to school, so I never had to worry if it went out of style. I couldn't drive it, so there went the worries about how it looked idling next to a new Ford Mustang. The love of my family provided me with peace of mind, happiness, and relief from fear. My connection to it was something right out of the 99% Realm. And because of this, I never felt alone.

My father compares the experience of the 99% Realm to those hazy moments when we are half awake and half asleep—when we are aware we are dreaming and trying desperately to hang onto that thread that connects us to the dream, but we know that if we yank too hard on the thread, we will lose the dream altogether. This is what it feels like when we lose even our brief connections to the Light. Disconnecting from the Light is the source of our unhappiness. Whenever we feel depressed, unfulfilled, or anxious, it's because we have lost touch with the 99% Realm. Just like the people of the kingdom, we are concerned, in those moments, with who is getting a milk bath and who isn't. And clearly, if it's not us, then there's a problem. Milk baths are a delightful pleasure of the 1% Realm and should be enjoyed whenever possible, but soul baths are what we are all really aiming for. Had my relationship with my family not allowed me to touch the Light, had it not been a consistent reminder of the nearness of 99% Realm, I might not have survived my teens-at least not in one emotional piece. If we focus on all the things from the 1% Realm that we are lacking—if we look at the material things we do have and the things we are missing as indications of who we are—we will never be happy for more than a few brief moments at a time. But if we trust that finding a way to access the Light is the path to unending happiness and constant joy, then we are on the path to having all our desires met.

The grass is NOT greener on the other side. Be careful not to use externals as a way to judge another's worth. Or your own.

Unless we apply conscious effort, the Light will come and go.

What most of us desire is intangible: love, peace, security, kindness. These exist in the 99% Realm.

The 1% Realm is home to our symptoms, or effects. The 99% Realm contains the cause.

Revealing the Light is the source of unending happiness and constant joy. Breaking with the Light is the source of all our unhappiness.

Consider the question, What does a human being truly desire from life? Then, after looking to your own life for answers, try to think in the broadest possible terms. If you think we all want McDonald's for dinner three times a week, or a personal copy of *The Matrix* on DVD, okay, write those down. But remember, you're trying to get at what we *truly* want from life—the desires that lie beneath our everyday desires. So instead of relying too heavily on your mind, let your heart speak. Now see what kind of list you come up with.

Take this list and compare it with the one you made in Chapter Two. In what ways are these lists of desires similar? In what ways are they different? Explore the ways in which your two sets of desires are pulling you in two potentially different directions. Which ones do you believe can be fulfilled by the 1% Realm and which by the 99% Realm? Mark each one accordingly. Make special note of any desire that appears on both lists. That is a great place to focus on as you continue through this book.

the purpose of your life is spiritual transformation—from a reactive being to a proactive being.

4

4

Before you begin this chapter, you might want to stretch a bit. Take a walk. Clear your head. Maybe do a few knee bends. Then get your favorite drink and settle into a comfortable chair. It's not that this chapter is more important than any of the others, but it does introduce a lot of key concepts to which you'll want to pay special attention.

First, let's take a closer look at two terms we encountered in the discussion of chaos theory in Chapter Two: reactive and proactive. You're being reactive when it feels as though things are happening to you. This is where most of us spend our time. It's exhausting, because you must constantly stay alert for whatever may *suddenly* happen next, and then hope you have what it takes to handle the situation skillfully.

When you are being reactive, you find yourself saying things like "If my teacher wasn't such a jerk, I would be getting a better grade in Spanish," which is like saying, *My teacher is the cause of my bad grade, not me.* "Billy just dumped me a week before the senior prom, and now my whole year is ruined" is another way of saying, *I'm not in control of my own moods.* "If I lived in a better neighborhood, or was skinnier, or had a girlfriend, or had a cooler car, then I'd be happy" is the equivalent of saying, *I give all of my power over to externals; they are in control of my happiness, not me.*

Reactive language is generated by our ego, which thrives on us handing our power over to it. Every time we use this sort of language we are making someone or something more powerful than us.

Playing the role of victim is a typical reactive behavior. When we're victims, we think the world is out to get us and at the same time think it owes us something; we gain a grandiose sense of entitlement. Sadly, this is because we feel incapable of doing anything for ourselves. We've given so much of our power away

life rules

chapter four: the purpose of your life is spiritual transformation—from a reactive being to a proactive being.

that we haven't anything left. But we don't see it that way. We perceive it as being cosmically picked-on: *I would have written an A paper, but my parents were fighting all night and I couldn't concentrate. I would be going out with Sharon tonight, except Mark asked her first. I should have been captain of the debate team, but that teacher hates me.*

On the other hand, when you take a proactive stance, *you* are happening to you. You are no longer waiting around to get hit by the result of some secret or random game being played by the universe. By being proactive, you've recognized that you are truly in charge. Proactive people know that if you can do something to make a situation better, then you do it—and if you can't, then you learn to accept it. As Helen Keller said, "So much has been given to me. I have no time to ponder that which been denied."

We'll return to the concepts of proactive and reactive later in this chapter, but for the moment, let's travel way back to an event that occurred before the dawn of time itself. Here we find ourselves in the presence of the Light, the boundless expression of God, whom kabbalists refer to as the Creator. This Light stretches into infinity, beyond time, space, or motion. The nature of this Light is to expand, impart, give, and share. (Make special note of this quality of sharing. It is important, and we'll revisit it soon.) The essence of the Light is *infinite* fulfillment, *boundless* joy, and *limitless* enlightenment. The breadth and nature of the Light are inconceivable, its extraordinary power lying beyond our limited comprehension. Think of the greatest love you have ever known; remember your most magnificent accomplishment; tap into your wildest fun, your biggest laugh ever, your best night's sleep, your most satisfying meal, your most amazing kiss. Pump them up like balloons at Macy's Thanksgiving Day Parade, and keep inflating them until they fill the whole sky. Then make them larger still, so that you can imagine them filling the universe and spilling over into universes that exist parallel to our own. You're still imagining only a tiny taste of the power of the Light.

life rules

chapter four: the purpose of your life is spiritual transformation—from a reactive being to a proactive being.

The Light's ever-expanding nature of giving and sharing is known as the First Cause.

To fulfill its desire to give, the Light creates a receiver. This is known as the First Effect, and it is considered the only true creation that has ever taken place. This receiver is called the Vessel, and because it was created by the Light, their essence is the same. The Vessel was not a literal vessel, something that you might be able to drink from. It was an energetic vessel that was capable of containing all that the Light shared with it. In the beginning, these were happy times. The Light was content to be sharing, and the Vessel was content to be receiving. This was because the nature of the Vessel was the Desire to Receive (in Aramaic, the word *Kabbalah* means "to receive"). Anything that the Vessel wanted—a-n-y-t-h-i-n-g—the Light would send its way. The Light's sharing of its essence with the Vessel led to a remarkable unity, which is called the Endless World, or what we refer to as the Endless. Within the Endless, it was impossible to tell where the Light ended and the Vessel began. Think of a cup carved out of ice into which water is being poured. The cup is the Vessel and the water the Light. In this example, both are composed of H2O, so at a molecular level it is impossible to distinguish one from the other. They are one essence in two forms. In much the same way, the Endless was total perfection—the Light completely sharing with the Vessel.

Because of their identical natures, the Vessel desired whatever it was that the Light was radiating forth. Imagine that if the Light was radiating stacks of $1,000 bills, the Vessel would find itself craving wealth. If the Light was generating apple orchards, the impulse for something crunchy and sweet would actualize within the Vessel. If the Light was throwing off sexual energy, the Vessel would suddenly have an itch to meet someone special. The Vessel's every desire was instantly sated. Can you think of a more optimal situation? For a long time, neither could the Vessel.

Before continuing, let's explore this Vessel more closely. When the Light created the Vessel, much of its nature flooded into the nature of the Vessel. The Light's basic nature is to share. The Vessel's basic nature is to receive, but in essence it contained both urges. Over time, the desire to share grew more profound. These two energies—sharing and receiving—correspond to male and female. Do you remember that in the introduction I discussed the code contained within Kabbalah—a code that helps us read The Bible more deeply? Well, here are our first two code words: Adam and Eve. Adam is the code word for our male energy, and Eve is the code word for our female energy.

This Vessel was our root, our origin. Every being—all the souls of humanity, past, present, and future—were contained within the Vessel. And like the Vessel, we too enter the world as babies aware only of our Desire to Receive. But as we grow older and peel back layers of our ego, or the curtain, we become aware that we also hold the Desire to Share.

One day the Vessel grew bored. Receiving and receiving and receiving had lost its thrill. Imagine going to the mall day after day after day and being given everything that you wanted. Oh, sure, the first couple of days would be fun. But eventually it would feel as though something was missing. The more the Light shared, the more of its nature entered the Vessel, and the more like the Light the Vessel became. Imagine hot water being poured into a cup made of ice. As the ice heated up, more and more attributes of the Light entered it, and soon the Vessel was aware not only of the Desire to Receive but also of the Desire to Share. This changed everything.

Let's take a moment here to think about sharing. There are many definitions of this word. Run through a few in your head. Is it sharing when the teacher tells you to give the kid behind you your extra pen because his pen is broken? Is it sharing when you help the little old lady across the street? Is it sharing when you

life rules

chapter four: the purpose of your life is spiritual transformation—from a reactive being to a proactive being.

tell your friend your deepest, darkest secret? Is it sharing when you tell *someone else* your friend's deepest, darkest secret? Is it sharing when you have family over for dinner? Is it sharing when you split your favorite candy bar with your boyfriend? Is it sharing when you split your *least* favorite candy bar with your boyfriend? Is it sharing when you give your friend some Ecstasy? Are you sharing when you're having sex? Think these through for a bit. Come up with a working notion of what you think sharing is. Remember, you need to test-drive everything in this book.

Now consider what it is that you need in order to share. What was the one factor linking all your examples of sharing? Most likely you needed to give something—emotionally, mentally, materially, or physically; you needed to be the cause. And only by being proactive can you be the cause.

Here is another key concept from this chapter: Bread of Shame. This is kind of a weird phrase, but its weirdness certainly makes it easy to remember! Bread of Shame is what we experience when everything is given to us and we are unable to earn any-thing for ourselves. In ancient times a wealthy man came across a poor man and invited him into his home so that he might share in some of his bread. The poor man hadn't had food for days, so ate greedily and with great appreciation. Yet, he could not shake the shame he felt at not having earned this bread himself. And eventually this shame began to interfere with his enjoyment of his meal. From that moment forward the poor man had direct realization of the shame he experienced around unearned bread, or what we now term Bread of Shame.

As we've noted, when we are born, we are able only to receive. But as we grow, so does our ability to earn what we receive. This concept is not difficult to grasp if you simply think about your own life. I'm sure you've known kids (in fact, you may be one) who had to complete chores around the house before they were given an allowance. These teens earned their allowances, and by doing so they earned a sense of fulfillment. And remember, fulfillment is what we are striving for. Now consider the kids you've known who were given their allowances automatically. They never had to help out around their homes, and perhaps they were even waited on by their parents or caregivers.

Both sets of kids ended up with money in their pockets, but those who didn't earn that money lacked the fulfillment of the other kids. Kids who don't have responsibilities are often referred to as "spoiled." This is actually the perfect word to describe them, because for such kids, the opportunity to become their own person has, quite literally, been *spoiled* for them. They may grow up feeling entitled, believing that everything should be given to them. But they will only become more and more dissatisfied, because they will not have earned what they've received. They become the Vessel—receivers only—and therefore earn Bread of Shame.

You can apply this to any aspect of your life. Think of how you've spent money that you earned yourself, as opposed to money that was given to you. Did one set of bills feel more precious in your pocket than the other? Were you inclined to hold onto the former longer? Did you spend the latter on things you didn't really need? How about the difference between receiving an A on a paper you practically wrote in your sleep and receiving a B+ on a paper you worked your butt off writing? Put aside your ego-driven desire for good grades and you'll find that the B+ paper was more fulfilling. How do you feel when your friends eat the birthday cake you bought at the deli, as compared with the one you made yourself? And how about when you get accepted by a top university because of your grades and your essay, but you get into another because both of your parents are alumni and generous contributors? Do you see a pattern here? When we are the cause, we can experience fulfillment; when we are the effect, we experience Bread of Shame.

This is not to say that you should never accept generosity. By all means do! By accepting another's kindness, you are helping them reduce their Bread of Shame, which is good for all involved. But be sure you accept with appreciation, and with the conscious knowledge that the other person has something they need to share. There is a balance to be achieved: For everything that we get, there is a payment. For instance, if your prosperous uncle buys you that guitar you've always wanted—the one that nobody in your family can afford—you clearly can't reciprocate in a financial way. But you can be mindful of your uncle's kindness and generosity. You can appreciate how well he knows you, as well as the fact that he spent his time earning the money to purchase the guitar, went to the store, discussed the various possibilities with the sales clerk, bought it, and carried it over to your place. You can appreciate the guitar both as a musical instrument you've been dying to play and as a gesture of love. Then think of your appreciation as your payment.

The same experience holds true for the Vessel. The Light was satisfying it on all levels, so the Vessel's existence was without struggle or effort. Imagine that instead of having to learn anything, you just know it all. There are no math classes, there is no swim team, and there is no after-school drama club. There is nothing to learn. You know everything. We're perfect at everything. And everyone else is as well. And the worst part of it is, it's all being done for you. You didn't lift a finger to set the table for the macaroni and cheese you had for dinner last night. You didn't have to scrape the plates when you were through or fight with your sister over whose turn it was to scrub the pots and pans. If you're a talented rapper, it has nothing to do with your emotional insights. If you're a whiz at science, it's not because you've studied hard. If you have to build a tree fort, there are no banged thumbs or hard-earned calluses—you build it perfectly the first time out. After a period of living in a world like this, you'd probably get angry and ask whoever it was that kept giving you everything—and I do mean everything—to please, please stop!

This is exactly what the Vessel did.

The Vessel had eternity to think things through. Although the Vessel valued all of the kindness being shown to it, it became clear what it wanted: (1) to be the cause of its own happiness; (2) to be the creator of its own fulfillment; (3) to share fulfillment with others; and (4) to control its own affairs.

The Vessel was experiencing Bread of Shame and all the negative emotions that accompany unearned good fortune. Because of this, it could no longer enjoy infinite fulfillment and absolute happiness. It needed to strike out on its own.

I once went to school with a boy whose parents had more money than anyone could ever spend. They had two apartments in Manhattan, a home in the Hamptons, another in Aspen, and still another in London. A chauffeur drove my classmate to school and picked him up again at the end of the day. A chef cooked his lunch. His clothes were impeccable. He traveled to fabulous countries. You get the picture: There was little the 1% Realm had to offer that he didn't have. But you may already have guessed that this boy was one of the most miserable kids I had ever met. His parents' money guaranteed him popularity, but he was moody, was often mean, and did poorly in school. Nothing seemed to matter to him; he didn't seem to understand the value of anything. And when his parents turned up at the occasional function, they behaved the same way. They had inherited their money too, and although they were beautifully dressed, there was no affection between them; they never touched or laughed at the same joke. They barely even spoke to one another.

Another boy I went to school with didn't have two nickels to rub together. His clothes were often shabby and his lunches meager. His father worked hard managing a grocery store where he had worked his way up from his first job as a bag boy. His mother was a receptionist at a local doctor's office. He took the bus to school or, during nice weather, walked. As often as possible, his mother turned up to walk him home. When his parents were together, there was lots of hugging and kissing—lots and lots of laughter and animated conversation. This family may have had little of what the 1% Realm has to offer, but what they did have they had earned, so they had little Bread of Shame. And they appreciated the value of what they had, which was each other.

This is not to say that the wealthy are villainous and the poor righteous—far from it. Money can be great! It's a wonderful means by which to share. Just make sure you are driving the money and the money isn't driving you. And the best way to do this is to earn it yourself. Have you ever dreamed of winning the lottery one day? Perhaps you already have plans for all the things you'd do with that money. It might surprise you to know that most people who win the lottery end up losing it all within a matter of years. Or their lives become a train wreck. One woman spent all of her winnings purchasing lottery tickets so that she could win more! Some have even committed suicide, when the Bread of Shame became too great.

How, then, can one do away with this terrible Bread of Shame? This leads to the final key word in this chapter: Resistance or Restriction. Getting back to the way things were before the birth of time, the Vessel decided that the only way to achieve its goal was to become proactive. So it decided to push back the Light. This is something we've all experienced—times when your parents have helped you too much with your homework, or a coach has walked you too carefully through a new sport. You know that in order to grow, you need to do it yourself, so you resist their help and set out to accomplish your goals on your own. Just recently Joey, a teen who visits our Kabbalah Centres, told me that he had grown so tired of his mother walking him to school in the morning—which she insisted on doing in order to keep him from being seduced by the gangs that hung out on the street corners—that he'd taken to sneaking out of his bedroom window and down the fire escape so that she couldn't follow him. None of this was easy for Joey, but his mother's protectiveness was actually inhibiting him from becoming his own cause—and he knew it. The moment the Vessel resisted the Light, the Light withdrew and created a vacant space. And by doing so, the infinite gave birth to the finite.

Naturally, the Light understood why the Vessel was taking such steps, and the Light lovingly gave the Vessel the time and space in which to evolve its own divine nature (just as Joey's mother eventually let Joey walk to school by himself, provided that he used the front door!). This time and space is the physical universe in which we currently find ourselves. In other words, the 1% Realm was created so that the Vessel could rid itself of its Bread of Shame—the very thing Joey was trying to do by sneaking down the fire escape.

A second result of the Vessel's Resistance was that the Adam and Eve energy separated from one another. These two segments then shattered into countless pieces that scattered throughout the universe. These are the tiny fragments of matter and energy that make up the cosmos from atoms to zebras, from microbes to musicians. Everything comes from the original Vessel, including you and me. Therefore, everything we can think of is imbued with its own spark of the Light, its own life force. Does this mean that even inanimate objects have souls? Rocks? Rivers? Fallen leaves? Yes, yes, and yes. The only difference between the soul of a rock and the soul of a rock star is the degree and intensity of their desire to receive the Light.

Once more, understanding the Vessel's desire for the opportunity to create its own fulfillment, the Creator disassembled the Endless World and transformed it into something like a picture puzzle. This allowed the Vessel to reassemble the puzzle of creation. Like the Vessel, we can now become creators of our fulfillment and the cause of our joy, thereby fulfilling our deepest desire and most profound need.

life rules

chapter four: the purpose of your life is spiritual transformation—from a reactive being to a proactive being.

To help illustrate this, let's say it's your kid brother's birthday. You search high and low for the perfect gift and finally decide on a puzzle of Rome, which is where he wants to live when he grows up. The puzzle has already been completed—in fact, the pieces are glued into place—and the result has been framed. You think it will look perfect at the foot of his bed so that he can see it every night before he goes to sleep. Yet while this may be a thoughtful gift, how much fulfillment will it actually give your brother? Three, four, five minutes. However long it takes to hang it on the wall, right? And that assumes he hangs it, and not you!

Now imagine giving him this same puzzle of Rome, but all 1,000 pieces are jumbled up in the box. You tell your brother that part of the present is that once he's finished it, you will have it framed for him so that he can hang it at the foot of his bed. He loves this idea and works diligently at it. It takes him nearly a month to complete, at the end of which you drive him to the store to pick out a frame. How much fulfillment does he have now? Do you see the difference? In the second scenario, you've given your brother what he really wanted more than anything else: the joy and accomplishment of building the puzzle himself.

After disassembling the Endless, the Creator produced a series of ten curtains. Each curtain reduced the Light, so that by the time the Light reached our physical world through the tenth and final curtain, it was reduced to near darkness. These ten curtains create ten distinct dimensions, which in Hebrew are called the Ten Sfirot (pronounced "sfeerote"). At the precise moment of the Vessel's shattering, the Ten Sfirot contracted in preparation for the birth of our universe. Six of the dimensions folded into one, which became known as the Upper World. Another piece of the code, they are the source of the phrase "six days of creation." Have you ever wondered why an all-powerful being needed six days to create what he could create faster than a sneeze? He didn't. The six days of creation are code for the uniting of the six dimensions. Of the remaining four, three are precursors to our three-dimensional universe, and the final one became the fourth dimension of space-time.

We are all trying to get back to the Light, back to unending happiness and constant joy. But this time we want to earn our keep. By embarking on this journey, we are ridding ourselves of our Bread of Shame.

The curtains were put into place by the Light. By dimming itself, the Light obscured many of its true attributes, and a series of dualities were introduced:

- If the Light exists on one side of a curtain, darkness must materialize on the other side.
- Likewise, if timelessness is the reality on one side of a curtain, the illusion of time is created on the other side.
- If there is perfect order on one side of the curtain, chaos exists in the other dimension.
- If there is wholeness and exquisite unity on one side of the curtain, then fragmentation and space and the laws of physics are on the other side.
- If cause and total fulfillment are on one side of the curtain, then effect and lack of fulfillment are on the other side.

Fortunately, although the Light is dimmed, it never truly goes away. It is still among us. If you cover a lamp with many layers of thin cloth, eventually the room will become dark, yet the lamp is still shining as brightly as ever. The intensity of its light remains unchanged. The only things that changed were the cloths covering the light. To gain more Light, we simply need to learn how to remove each layer of cloth. But it is wise to do so slowly. We've all had the experience of walking from a dark movie theater into bright sunlight. It can be blinding if you're not prepared. The goal of this book is to help you remove layers of cloth, and to prepare you for presence of the Light.

If any of this sounds familiar, it may be because you've been learning about the Big Bang and Superstring Theory in physics. The similarities between the discoveries of modern science and the ancient teachings of Kabbalah are uncanny. But whereas science is focused more on the hows of physical reality, Kabbalah addresses the whys.

Let's look first at the Big Bang, which scientists today might describe in the following way:

> Approximately 15 billion years ago, before the universe came into existence, there was nothing. No time. No space. The universe began in a single point. This point was surrounded by nothingness. It had no width. No depth. No length. This speck contained the whole of space, time, and matter. The point erupted into an explosion of unimaginable force, expanding at the speed of light like a bubble. This energy eventually cooled and coalesced into matter—stars, galaxies, and planets.

Compare that with this excerpt from the writings of 16th-century Kabbalist Rav Isaac Luria:

> The universe was created out of nothingness from a single point of light. This nothingness is called the Endless World. The Endless World was filled with infinite Light. The Light was then contracted to a single point, creating primordial space. Beyond this point nothing is known. Therefore, the point is called the beginning. After the contraction, the Endless World issued forth a ray of Light. This ray of Light then expanded rapidly. All matter emanated from that point.

Pretty amazing, right? How about this description of superstring theory by the prominent scientist Brian Greene:

> Just as the vibration patterns of a violin string give rise to different musical notes, the different vibration patterns of a fundamental string give rise to different masses and force charges. String theory also requires extra space dimensions that must be curled up to a very small size to be consistent with our never having seen them.

It's no coincidence that the number of dimensions required to make the theory work (ten) and the number of dimensions condensed into one (six) are identical to the numbers given by the ancient kabbalists.

Dr. Michio Kaku, another leading proponent of Superstring Theory, wrote the following:

> The Universe is a symphony of vibrating strings. And when strings move in ten-dimensional space-time, they warp the space-time surrounding them in precisely the way predicted by general relativity. Physicists retrieve our more familiar four-dimensional universe by assuming that, during the Big Bang, six of the ten dimensions curled up into a tiny ball, while the remaining four expanded explosively, giving us the Universe we see.

Let's return to the Vessel, which, by pushing back the Light, has taken a substantial proactive step—one to which we can relate in many ways. I certainly can. All my life I've struggled with attention deficit disorder, or what's known as ADD. After 10 or 15 minutes, my attention span is shot. If I'm sitting, I need to stand up and walk. If I'm walking around, I need to pop into a store or stop and examine a tree or a flower. At the office, I have various toys on my desk to occupy my hands while I work. When I was going to school, this was a big problem. Not only could I not hold my focus, but one of the side effects was that I felt disconnected from everything and everyone. It was yet another piece of why I didn't fit in.

I remember my very first day of kindergarten, standing on the playground with my father. I held his hand tight and watched all the other kids playing together and having fun. I couldn't figure out why they weren't playing with *me*. This is a painful memory, but I later realized that all I needed to do was go and play with them! My classmates were already in the midst of play, already engaged in fun. I was waiting for them to "happen" to me rather than being proactive and introducing myself to them.

The concept of children at play is not a bad analogy for the Light, and my standing there is not unlike the way all of us, at one time or another, stand on the outskirts of joy and fulfillment, wondering why it isn't coming to us! Certainly, over the years, my parents and various teachers tried to help me negotiate the difficult terrain of ADD. And while I appreciated their guidance, my situation didn't truly begin to change until I started to take responsibility for my circumstances. I forced myself to talk to people at school even though I was deathly afraid. My fear wasn't shyness—it came from living in a complete disconnection from my surroundings. Most of the time, the kids I spoke with had no idea what I was going through, but it didn't matter, because the process at that point was about healing myself. Often I would need to skip class, because I had learned firsthand that being there was pointless without being able to focus. I would go for long walks and consider the various aspects of Kabbalah that my father was teaching me. I began to challenge the notion that life was happening to me—that I had been dealt a rotten hand—and started to reshape my life into something positive.

By taking responsibility for my own situation, I was able to bring it into perspective. Sure, I struggled with ADD (as well as dyslexia), but everyone struggles with something—much of it far worse

life rules

chapter four: the purpose of your life is spiritual transformation—from a reactive being to a proactive being.

than what I was dealing with. There is always good and bad. And remember, when the Vessel had only "good," it eventually rebelled. Good means nothing if you don't earn it yourself and you are unable to share it. As I looked around me, I saw plenty of kids who had no learning disabilities, but who came from homes where their parents fought all the time, or where a sibling had died tragically, or where a parent drank too much. Like a resident in the kingdom of complainers, I wasn't altogether thrilled with my lot in life—but when I considered it from all angles, it wasn't so bad at all. Plus, my ADD contained a hidden treasure: It kept me out of trouble.

Even more than Kabbalah, ADD contributed to my outcast status at school. Kids wrote me off as shy and odd, which is why I wasn't the first person they thought of when there was a new drug to try, or when someone's brother bought a keg of beer, or when they drove a new car at top speed down the highways that flanked New York City. Without my knowing it, my ADD kept me safe.

There is always a reason for everything. Often, especially in the beginning, we may not know the reason, but that doesn't mean it doesn't exist. Someone who is afflicted with acne as a teenager may feel lonely, frustrated, and depressed. *Why me?* they may think. *Why can't I have clear skin like everyone else?* Yet this acne may have saved that teenager from a painful experience. It may have kept him from casual sex that might have resulted in an unwanted pregnancy or perhaps a sexually transmitted disease. These would have been far worse than the acne, although at the time, nothing could have felt worse than inflamed skin.

The more I was able to be proactive about my ADD, the easier it became to work with, and the more joyful my life became. I had a rich home life, and while my days at school were troubled, I was always able to fit into my family—even though my house was often full of strangers whom my parents had taken in. Eventually I was able to transform my struggles into positive energy—energy I could share with others who were struggling through painful situations of their own.

When we look into the 99% Realm, we discover four key attributes of the Light that we need to express in our world in order to remove Bread of Shame. These aspects are already within us, as the Light shared them with us before the dawn of time. They are what we will uncover each time we shut down our ego and remove a curtain. These are the attributes of being proactive:

- Being the Cause;
- Being a Creator;
- Being in Control;
- Sharing.

The world is not something that just happens to us. It is something we make happen. And right now—right this very second, as you read this sentence—you are shaping the environment that determines every aspect of your life. Doing so with mindfulness, love, and compassion can only bring you that much closer to the Light.

Conversely, the traits of the Vessel are reactive:

- Being the Effect;
- Being a Created Entity;
- Being Under the Control of Everything;
- Receiving.

Reactive behavior is founded on the human Desire to Receive—the original desire created in the Endless World. Reactive behavior includes anger, envy, overconfidence, low self-esteem, greed, and animosity. In truth, 99% of our behavior is reactive. So what can you do about it? Become the cause in a way that involves sharing.

○ If things feel as if they are happening to you, as if you are not the cause but the effect, then you are being reactive.

○ If you are in charge, if you are the cause, then you are being proactive.

○ The Light existed before time. It is a manifestation of the Creator and has power beyond anything we can imagine. Its ever-expanding nature of giving and sharing is known as the First Cause. Its basic nature is the Desire to Share.

○ The Vessel was created by the Light in order to receive its benevolent nature. This is known as the First Effect. Its basic nature is the Desire to Receive.

The union of the Vessel and the Light created the Endless.

Because the Vessel was created by the Light, its essence grew to contain both the Desire to Receive and the Desire to Share.

Bread of Shame occurs when you are receiving without having earned it.

In order to rid itself of Bread of Shame, the Vessel resisted the Light. This created the 1% Realm. It also shattered the Vessel into countless tiny pieces. We all contain an aspect of the Light.

○ The Creator shaped the Endless into a puzzle, which the Vessel may reassemble and thereby earn fulfillment.

○ Ten curtains (*Sfirot*) were erected to separate the 1% Realm from the Light. During the Vessel's Resistance, six of these folded into one.

○ Modern Big Bang and Superstring Theories are remarkably similar to kabbalistic beliefs with regard to the creation of the universe.

○ Taking responsibility for your circumstances in life is the first step toward proactive behavior.

○ The Desire to Share is already within us; we just need to shut down our ego—or remove the curtains—so that we can access it.

Make a list of all the most notable times parents, teachers, relatives, friends, or even passing acquaintances have done something for you—with the best of intentions—that made your life easier. Now consider how those times made you feel. Cared for and appreciated, perhaps, but did any of these moments contain an underlying desire to take care of it yourself? Did any of them make you feel as if you were being controlled, as if you couldn't do things for yourself, as if you were the effect of decisions and choices rather than the cause? Did their actions in any way undermine your ability to care for yourself? List ways in which the situation might have been more enjoyable and beneficial for you. Do any of these include taking a more active role in your own success or pleasure?

in moments of transformation, we make contact with the 99% realm.

5

5

life rules

chapter five: in moments of transformation, we make contact with the 99% realm.

grew up a fan of New York Knicks basketball. Watching Patrick Ewing and Mark Jackson double-team their opponents seemed liked heaven on earth. My brother and I would watch every single game on television. And every once in a while we'd be given tickets for the real thing.

But despite my love for the Knicks, it was my team's nemesis, Michael Jordan of the Chicago Bulls, who first taught me about transformation. Watching him play, I knew beyond a doubt that he'd made contact with the 99% Realm. It was a beautiful sight to behold when Michael Jordan defied the laws of gravity, leaping, hanging in the air, and shooting the ball in ways that didn't seem humanly possible. And as much as I wept for my home team, I was mesmerized by his talents. Right before our very eyes, he was connecting to the 99%, and I wanted to get plugged in as well.

But I was just me, stuck in a school full of kids who didn't understand me, and most of whom I didn't understand any better. The only things I had in my court were my family and Kabbalah. But the older I grew, the more I realized how potent these things were.

This chapter is about the moment we decide how we are going to act—the moment when transformation is possible. Believe it or not, there is actually a millisecond of possibility before each decision we make, even for those decisions that seem instantaneous. And if we train our minds to respond in that moment with the Desire to Share (proactive) rather than the Desire to Receive (reactive), our lives will begin to take on a more positive shape. Every time we resist a reaction, we have transformed a particular aspect of ourselves. When Michael Jordan was on the court, I'm sure he was aware of everyone else's actions, but he never seemed to react to them. Rather, he proactively implemented his own strategy, and by doing so he elevated his own game as well as that of his teammates.

life rules

chapter five: in moments of transformation, we make contact with the 99% realm.

Let's revisit cause and effect for a moment. Whenever we react to external events, we become nothing more than an effect of whatever that external event may be. A driver in the next lane shouts at us, and we shout back. This behavior leaves us stuck where the Vessel was stuck so long ago. By shifting our attention to transforming that energy through personal growth, we become creators. We become the cause. And by becoming the cause, we are no longer swayed by outside forces, positive or negative. We have gained control. And control of our own lives is great! It means we can choose to share. When we forget or refuse to share—when we rely solely on receiving—we are gratifying our ego. And, knowingly or not, we are making sure every layer of the curtain remains snugly in place. Our ego is our ignorance. It thrives on reactive behavior because when we are reacting to something, we are all about "me"—and that is what keeps us from the Light.

I'm not talking about healthy ego here—the part of you that takes pleasure in being praised for baking that delicious batch of brownies for your friends, or the satisfaction you take in seeing a short story of yours in print, or in standing up to the guy who's been bullying your kid brother. I'm talking about the ego that thinks that whenever it rains, it's wrecking *your* day (even though it's raining on the entire city). Or if your brother doesn't want to help you with your homework, it's because he's mad at you or doesn't care enough about you—not because he might have had a rotten day at school or is tired. This is the ego that makes us believe that we are the center of the universe, and that everything revolves around us.

Earlier we discussed how all of us are striving to reduce our own suffering and find our own happiness. The problem is that we often mistakenly interpret the actions of others as anti-me, when in fact they are merely pro-them—meaning they have nothing to do with us. The less personally we can take things, the happier we will be. If the subway is running late, it's not just happening

life rules

chapter five: in moments of transformation, we make contact with the 99% realm.

to us. We are not the sole reason the subway exists. If your father won't let you use the car, this doesn't mean you are being treated unfairly; other people need to use that car as well. The car does not exist solely for you. Some years ago, a scientific study revealed that people who used the words *me*, *my*, and *mine* a lot suffered a high rate of heart attacks! That's because their hearts were too caught up in ego instead of opening and sharing!

Our ego expects to receive. Our ego gets us into trouble. We need to control that ego. We need to stop letting it roll through our lives, tricking us into reacting to things. Experiment with resisting your ego, and see what happens. Start in small places with small steps. Understand that what you are undertaking is not easy. Ego will creep up on you when you least expect it. And it will fight back when you try to set it aside. After all, it likes being the center of attention! So be patient with yourself. Be kind to yourself. Every step forward counts, even a baby one—and if you get frustrated because you are not moving fast enough, that's just your ego getting the upper hand. We are learning to love our neighbors as we love ourselves. So pay special attention to loving yourself. Remember, you can't put the oxygen mask on someone else until your own mask is securely in place!

A young woman, Sarah, who had been coming to one of our Kabbalah Centres for years, once shared a painful story with me about resisting her ego. She lived with her mother and her mother's boyfriend, Duane. Duane used to beat her mother regularly, but her mother refused to leave him. Sarah said that her mother loved Duane and believed that over time she could calm him down. One day Sarah came home from school to find her mom lying on the kitchen floor unconscious, covered in blood. At first, Sarah thought her mother was dead. At the hospital the doctors told Sarah that her mother had a broken arm, two broken legs, and a crushed rib and had also sustained damaged to her head, but they wouldn't know more about her chances for a full recovery until she woke up.

life rules

chapter five: in moments of transformation, we make contact with the 99% realm.

Sarah was devastated—and incredibly angry. Her father had given her mom a gun for protection years ago, and Sarah knew just where her mother kept it. So Sarah loaded it and went to look for Duane. Sure enough, she found him outside his favorite bar, flirting with a woman. Sarah hid behind a tree.

"I had him in my sights," Sarah told me. "I could have shot him so easily, and I felt that was the right thing to do." Then she remembered what she had been studying in her Kabbalah classes, and she forced herself to pause. Instantly she realized that by standing there with the gun aimed at Duane—however powerful she might feel—she had actually given her power away. She was merely the effect, and he was the cause. And as soon as she realized this, she lowered the gun and returned home.

"Had I fired that shot," she said, "I would have given away so much of my power that being the cause would have been much harder to achieve."

In the moment Sarah decided not to fire the shot, she revealed the Light to herself and to the world.

The steps laid out in this book will serve you well for a lifetime. That's the good news. It's also true that by the end of the week, or the month, or even the year, you won't have them all under your belt. The process of transformation will also last a lifetime. So don't expect to "get it over with." That's not the nature of the commitment you're making. Just start where you are, not where you think you should be, and move at a comfortable pace.

Here's one important thing to keep in mind about reacting: It's easy. And because it's easy, it gives us Bread of Shame, which is exactly the opposite of what we are striving for. Whether we react passively or aggressively makes no difference. As long as we slip into our natural tendency in any given situation, we are relinquishing our free choice. Within the 1% Realm, our free choice consists solely of being reactive or being proactive. This is a really big idea, so take your time, and think it through. If you're like me, you may think that most aspects of your life involve free choice: You can eat hot dogs or a veggie burger, you can wear silk or corduroy, you can brush your teeth or go directly to bed, and so on. But in each case, you are not making a choice at all; you are just satisfying a desire, and hence you are the effect. Whether you eat hot dogs or go for the burger isn't the point. You are an effect of your hunger. Your free choice comes into play when you choose to restrict that desire—or not.

When we react to something, we are tapping into our animal nature. As far as we know, animals are not able to access that split second before a response. Their desires are compulsive, and their reactions are as well; they go for the instant gratification. When we pause first or restrict our response, however, we are tapping into our God nature. We are choosing to no longer be the effect of our desire. Instead, we are choosing to be the cause. Restriction, by the way, doesn't mean that we won't decide to satiate that desire after all. It just means that we pause and make a conscious decision.

I knew lots of kids in high school who were bored with life. This wasn't unusual. For one reason or another, most teens fall prey to boredom! Some of the boys turned to drugs and alcohol, and it worked temporarily. There was no Restriction here; their behavior was simply the effect of their desire. Eventually these kids burned out. Instant gratification draws the Light so quickly that it's unsustainable. Therefore, those who exercise it are not creating anything that will last them for the rest of their lives.

There was another group of kids who responded to their boredom differently. They constricted their desire for instant excitement and instead began to consider what they could do that would contribute to society as well as improve their lives. By becoming involved in community service or taking part-time jobs, these kids became the cause. By restricting their desire, they were able to respond proactively. And by doing so, they were revealing Light that they would carry with them always.

Let's say you are waiting for your date in a restaurant. You're wearing your favorite dress or your favorite khakis and button-down shirt. You took some time to get ready. And you're excited, because although you don't yet know this person all that well, you like him or her. About 15 minutes after the time set for dinner, your cell phone rings. It's your date, canceling.

When I use this scenario in a class that I'm teaching, student reactions vary considerably. One student might say she would order a drink and flirt with the first single guy she sees. She is looking to punish her date for canceling on her. Another might order a huge meal and overeat. He is punishing himself. Another might cry, feeling hurt and insignificant.

Each of these responses is a reaction to the phone call. Do you see that? None of them are self-generated. My students are turning their reaction either outward (by seeking revenge) or inward (by overeating). Rarely does anyone say, "If my date didn't show up, perhaps there was a good reason for it. And if there wasn't, then I'm delighted not to have spent more time in that relationship. That person isn't right for me. I am the Light, and I am glad not to be disconnected from the Light by an unhealthy relationship."

By being proactive, we are resisting our knee-jerk reaction to an event or a series of events. The more effectively we are able to resist, the more we open to the Light.

Let's be honest: Part of the reason we react to things is the instant gratification we get. If we react with anger, we might feel better after blowing off steam. If we react manipulatively,

life rules

chapter five: in moments of transformation, we make contact with the 99% realm.

perhaps we'll enjoy the feeling of being in control. If we react happily, we will most likely enjoy a flush of pleasure. And in those moments, good or bad, when we generate that flickering potent energy, we are connecting with the 99% Realm. But momentarily connecting with the 99% Realm does not necessarily promise that we are revealing the Light or gaining fulfillment in any long-lasting or meaningful way. When our desires are immediately fulfilled, more often than not we experience Bread of Shame, and we burn out.

Keep in mind that reacting can feel "positive." For instance, when someone compliments me on a new haircut or likes something that I wrote, this can make me feel good—but in these examples, the other person is the cause and our good feelings are merely the effect. Therefore our happiness will be temporary. We also run the risk of finding ourselves becoming dependent on compliments or praise in order to experience happiness. A rush of external happiness is as dangerous as a rush of external anger.

Remember, we are struggling to become our own cause. This is not to say that we won't have responses to situations, that good or bad things will happen around us to which we'll remain oblivious. We're not aspiring to a life like the one depicted in *The Stepford Wives*; emotions will always arise as long as we live. What we are trying to do is hone our ability to recognize our emotions when they do come up, and to train our minds to work within that pause before we would reflexively react.

Momentary connections with the Light, when brought about by external factors, give us brief glimpses into the potential of profound transformation—but the only way to hold onto that magic is to resist our reactive behavior mindfully and consistently. Let's examine how true transformation might look. First scenario: One hundred thousand dollars in small bills lies on top of a desk in a business office. A man walks in and sees the money. After mak-

life rules

chapter five: in moments of transformation, we make contact with the 99% realm.

ing sure no one is watching, he scoops up the cash and flees like a bandit.

Second scenario: A man walks in and sees the same small mountain of cash. He gets very nervous being near all that money, begins shaking, and flees the building like a scared rabbit.

Third scenario: A man walks in and sees the money. He checks to see that no one is looking. Then he scoops up the cash and begins to run. But then he stops. He agonizes for a moment and decides to return the money to the desk.

Fourth scenario: A man walks in and sees the money. He takes it and places it inside a briefcase. He locks the briefcase and hands it over to the authorities for safekeeping. He leaves a note on the desk that informs whoever has misplaced a large sum of cash to contact him, and he will direct that person to the authorities to retrieve the money.

Which man's behavior do you think most closely resembles what you might do? Consider what we have learned so far. Which scenario reveals more spiritual Light? In which situation is the man the cause and not the effect? Which man expresses the most spiritual Light in his own life? The answer may surprise you. Let's examine each man's actions.

First scenario: In this case, the man is governed by his reactive, instinctive Desire to Receive, which tells him to take the money and run. Because of his reactive behavior, he does not receive the Light of fulfillment in his life. He is the effect, not the cause, and he will therefore have Bread of Shame.

Second scenario: This man is merely reacting to his instinctive desire to be frightened. Reacting to his natural instinct produces no Light. The man enters the building and leaves it again with his nature unchanged.

life rules

chapter five: in moments of transformation, we make contact with the 99% realm.

Third scenario: This man initially reacts to his desire to steal the cash, but then, in that all-important moment before a choice is made, he stops. He shuts his reaction down proactively. Then, going against his initial instinct, and transforming his nature in this one instant, he returns the money. He makes himself the cause, the director of his own destiny—not the effect of a suit-case full of money! His transformation from reactive to proactive reveals spiritual Light.

Fourth scenario: This man merely reacts to his instinctive desire to do the right thing. He was already in a proactive state of mind concerning stealing the money. No change of nature occurs. He remains the same person throughout the situation. Such behavior produces no additional Light in this person's life, according to Kabbalah. The honorable man in this scenario does have an opportunity to reveal Light, however. After returning the money, he must not react to his ego, which tells him he is kind and virtuous. He must resist his Desire to Receive—which in this case means his desire to receive praise for his good deed. He must realize that the great opportunity for him lies not in the physical act of returning the money, but rather in keeping his good deed secret and rejecting self-praise.

Remember that our positive traits do not reveal the Light. The Light that has already been revealed from previously transform-ing your reactive behavior into proactive or positive behavior does not go away. It is filling your Vessel, and it is safe. But new Light is revealed only when we identify, uproot, and transform our reactive negative characteristics. It is *the degree of change* in our nature that determines the measure of our fulfillment.

Here's an updated version of a traditional kabbalist tale, "The Wise Man and the Ten Thieves," to further illustrate this point Ike the mail carrier lived in a small town in the Midwest. He and his wife Cathy had only one child, a son named David. When David turned seven, he was stricken with a mysterious illness.

With each passing day, the young boy grew weaker. Ike drove hundreds of miles to visit countless doctors, but to no avail. Cathy could see in her little boy's eyes that time was running out. She could sense the angel of death hovering over his bedroom. Little David desperately needed a miracle.

It so happened that a wise old man lived in the same town. He was not a doctor, but local people came to him with ailments that resisted a cure; it was rumored that he could talk to angels and perform all kinds of wonders. Ike's last option was to pay a visit to the old sage.

When he learned of young David's heartrending situation, the wise man was greatly saddened. Ike begged him to do something in the way of prayer and blessings. The healer took Ike's hand in his and promised to do the best he could.

That night the old mystic ascended high into the spirit world, using secret prayers and meditations known only to a few. When he reached the gates of heaven, he was stunned to find that the gates were locked. The fate of the little boy had already been settled.

The night soon passed, and the morning sun began to rise in the eastern sky over this quaint Midwestern town. Ike and the old sage met outside the post office. Sorrowfully, the old man gave the mail carrier his news.

"I'm afraid there is nothing I can do," the sage said. "It has already been decreed that the gates of heaven remain locked to your only son."

Ike was shattered. Tears began streaming down his face as he begged the old man to try one more time. "I have nowhere else to turn!" cried Ike. "David is my only son, my only child. And you are my only hope!"

Not having the heart to deny this tormented man, the old mystic replied, "I cannot promise anything. But I will make one more attempt."

And at that moment a bizarre idea occurred to him. Quickly summoning his young assistant, Thomas, he made a peculiar request. "Please go at once to the nearest city," the mystic said, "and bring to me ten hardened criminals. No less than ten."

Thomas was shocked, but he knew better than to question the man who could talk to angels.

"Find me burglars, looters, the worst scoundrels possible," the old man added. "And please, hurry!"

Thomas drove into the city, and to his surprise, he was able to gather together ten thieves quite quickly. In fact, he was amazed at how readily they agreed to accompany him to the home of his master. Even these villains had heard of the mysterious healer in the not-so-distant town who possessed extraordinary powers.

Thomas and this sordid band arrived at the house of the mystic, who thanked them for coming and invited them all into his home. Some of the nastiest criminals in the country sat around his living room, boastfully recounting their favorite crime stories. Then the old man motioned for them to be silent. They all listened respectfully as the old man who could perform miracles, the healer who could cure the most terrible ailments, asked these wily thieves to share his prayers.

The next morning, at the break of dawn, as roosters crowed and a sweet-scented summer breeze blew ever so gently, Ike the mail carrier danced wildly down Main Street, looking like the happiest man on earth.

life rules

chapter five: in moments of transformation, we make contact with the 99% realm.

A car pulled up alongside the ecstatic man. Thomas was at the wheel. In the back seat was the old sage. "My dear friend," he exclaimed, "it appears by your delighted face and your dancing shoes that you have good news to share."

"I thank you with all my heart!" cried the mail carrier. "My beautiful boy David received a miracle overnight. It's as though he was never sick. He is out milking the cows right now, doing chores as we speak!"

"Indeed, this is very good news," said the man who could talk to angels. "Be well, my friend!" The old sage then drove off.

Puzzled, Thomas turned to his mentor in the back seat. "How can this be?" he asked him. "Those men I brought to you yesterday . . . they were burglars, safecrackers, and muggers. Thieves. Why did you pray with such shady characters?"

And this is how the sage replied:

"When I prayed that first night for our friend and his only son, I saw that the gates of heaven were locked. There was nothing I could do. The poor man's heart was shattered. How could I refuse him when he pleaded with me to try again? Then a thought came to me. So I asked you to bring me that assortment of villains, which you did. Then last night I prayed again, but the gates of heaven were still locked."

Thomas was confused. "So what happened?" he asked. "How did you cure his son if the gates remained locked?"

The mystic broke into a wide smile. "Ah, but this time I had a band of thieves to assist me." He replied. "You see, Thomas, a good thief knows all about breaking and entering. I brought them on my journey and they picked all the locks! These criminals broke into heaven, and that is how my prayers were able to make their way into the heavenly sanctuary."

life rules

chapter five: in moments of transformation, we make contact with the 99% realm.

The car continued on. It was still early, but the small town's streets were coming to life. And if you knew where to look, you might have seen a number of professional criminals, intermingled among the honest townspeople, discreetly tipping their hats to the healer's car as it passed by.

I love this story. The mystic is the embodiment of our soul, of all our positive qualities. The thieves represent all of our negative, egocentric traits. After all, we are all thieves to one degree or another. As we see in the story, our good qualities are not enough in themselves to provide all the answers to our prayers. Rather, it's our negative attributes that provide the master keys to heaven. When we identify and work to transform our self-centered qualities, the key turns and the gates unlock. Blessings and good fortune are now free to rain down upon us.

Another lesson to be found here lies in the willingness of the sage to keep trying even when all seemed lost. When practicing transformation, don't be afraid of failing. We actually reveal more Light for ourselves and for the world when we fall and then get up again. If we never fall, we stay exactly where we are. And while time may move us forward physically, spirituality we never advance. Failing may batter our self-esteem, triggering depression or anxiety, which are natural reactions to a difficult situation. But respond by being kind to yourself. Try not to beat yourself up. In fact, celebrate having fallen!

Michael Jordan could have been a good basketball player without plugging into the 99% Realm. His game would have been impressive, but without challenging himself to resist the easy shot, the easy reaction to another player's move, would he have blown our minds? When I was young, Michael Jordan was one of the few things that made sense to me. And he got me wondering not only how I could tap into the 99% Realm myself, but how I could make it last.

○ There is a moment before every decision we make where we can choose whether we want to respond proactively or reactively.

○ Our ego thrives on reactive behavior; it gets to be the center of attention!

○ Contrary to the ego's message, the world does not revolve around us. Try to remember this at all times!

○ By transforming our behavior from reactive to proactive—from being the effect to being the cause —we receive the Light of fulfillment.

○ Don't be afraid to fall. Rising up again generates greater Light than if we'd never fallen.

Divide a page into four columns—you'll probably want to use the paper lengthwise. In the first column, write down three recent instances in which you reacted to a person or a situation. In the second column, jot down what emotions were triggered by each experience. And in the third column, make note of how you behaved in each situation. What was your reaction? In this exercise, you are homing in on your "easy" response, your instinctive reaction. Now that you see your behavior spelled out before you, consider ways in which you could act proactively in the future. Write some of those thoughts down in column four.

chapter six:

never—and that means never—lay blame on other people or external events.

6

6

L et's just jump right in here. Say you've just recently gotten your driver's license, and you've taken the family car to go visit a friend. You arrive safely, for which you commend yourself—but while you're driving back home, it starts to snow. At first the snow is light, and with both hands on the wheel in the 10-and-2 position, you're doing fine. Then the snow starts falling harder and harder. Still, with hands in place and full concentration, you know you can get home in time to watch your favorite TV show and impress your parents. You are almost there, sliding a little along the twisting turns near your home, when suddenly you hit a pothole. Your car spins out of control and crashes into an oncoming vehicle. Fortunately no one is hurt, but everyone is shaken up. *There was a pothole*, you tell the woman whose car you hit. *A big, gaping pothole!* Your parents are not impressed. You are grounded for a month and not allowed to drive for two. *But there was a pothole!*

Nice try.

Yes, there was a pothole. Life is packed with potholes. Sometimes there are several waiting for us in the course of one afternoon. But if we keep blaming the potholes—if we keep pointing to them and shouting, *it's not my fault*—we will be unable to connect with the Light. When it began to snow, you could have pulled off the road and waited to see if the weather cleared; snowfalls are often brief. When you hit the twisty road close to home, you could have pulled into a gas station and called a family member to come and get you, and then picked up the car the next day.

Each moment of that drive home contained a choice—not necessarily a choice that you liked (and certainly not a choice your ego liked), but a choice nonetheless. Be sure to recognize that you chose to finish the drive home at that particular time without calling home for help. This is not necessarily a "wrong" decision. In fact, according to Kabbalah, there is no right and wrong;

life rules

chapter six: never—and that means never—lay blame on other people or external events.

there are only different outcomes. There's every possibility that if that pothole hadn't turned up, you would have made it home safe and sound. But when the pothole does appear, recognize that your choices led you to that situation, so *you and you alone* are responsible for the outcome.

Although taking responsibility for your actions may cause you some discomfort at first, in the long run you will be amazed at how life-altering it can be. If you are responsible for your mistakes, you have the power to change them and to transform yourself. If you are not responsible for your mistakes—if there are always mitigating circumstances, or if someone or something else is always responsible—then what chance do you have of improving your life? If something external is causing your suffering, then it's externals that have to change in order for your suffering to cease. And, as we've seen, we can't always control our externals—in which case there's not much you can do but wait around for your luck to turn.

This is how many of us approach our lives—by waiting to be dealt a better hand. But as you've read in this book, life does not happen to you; you happen to you! One of the most concrete ways of experiencing this is to begin to take responsibility for exactly the way your life looks and feels right at this moment. This is not an opportunity to judge yourself and find yourself lacking. Rather, it is an opportunity to begin to truly get to know yourself. The more you own up to your vulnerabilities and mistakes, the more fodder you will have with which to transform. Remember what we learned in the last chapter—that our positive actions do not earn us the Light or the fulfillment we seek. Rather, the Light is revealed to us by transforming our negatives. So rather than pretend your negatives don't exist, embrace them. Then transform them.

Check in with your thoughts right this second. You're probably thinking something like "But I know I could be happy if only

_____" (fill in the blank). This is just another way of blaming the externals. Something external is being withheld from you by a parent, a friend, or life in general, and this is what is keeping you from experiencing the life you deserve. With this sort of thinking, you are constantly making something or somebody else the cause, thereby reducing yourself to the effect.

If something goes wrong in your life and you recognize your responsibility in it, you are also recognizing yourself as the cause. Okay, great. Now that we have that in place, we can actually do some good, deep within ourselves. So let's explore a little further. We've all grown up playing games. No matter where you are from—no matter what your socioeconomic background or your ethnicity—your childhood included various kinds of games, and the object of these games was to win. When you won, you had a palpable sense of satisfaction, whereas when your opponent won, you were disappointed. It was all about the winning!

But was it really? Let's go back to the Vessel for a moment. In one sense, the Vessel just kept winning and winning and winning. Yet Bread of Shame kept accumulating, since by not earning the wins, the Vessel was not the cause and therefore provided no fulfillment or lasting joy. The Vessel had to decide to resist the Energy in order to earn its wins. The same holds true for us. Imagine being on a team where it has been agreed upon by all parties that your team will consistently win. The players will compete and fans will attend, but there is absolutely no doubt that you will win every single time. How do you think you might feel?

Bored, frustrated, or even angry? Without the risk of losing, winning means nothing. In order to experience a fair fight, you need a worthy opponent. In Kabbalah, the opponent is called the Satan (accent on second syllable, suh-*tahn*). You may be asking yourself, are we talking about the devil? This book has made a lot of sense up until now. But the guy with the horns and the pitchfork? I don't think so!

life rules

chapter six: never—and that means never—lay blame on other people or external events.

That Satan you're imagining is the product of superstition and commercialization. The Satan I'm talking about is another one of our code words. This is the code word for reactive behavior, which we were discussing in Chapter Five. Two thousand years ago, the major text of Kabbalah, known as *The Zohar*, revealed the Opponent, or the Satan. It even identified some of the Opponent's weapons and strategies. He is the unseen cause of chaos in the physical world and in the human spirit. He is the one who points our accusatory fingers at one another. If we are feeling anxious, overwhelmed, fearful, uncertain, pessimistic, depressed, angry, jealous, or doubtful, the Satan is the one behind it all.

If we hear a voice egging us on to do something we know we absolutely shouldn't do, that voice belongs to the Opponent. So does the voice that encourages us to pull back from an action we absolutely know we should take. And, worst of all, it is his voice that shrewdly talks us out of applying resistance and ridding ourselves of our reactive behavior once and for all. By ridding ourselves of our reactive behavior, we are ridding ourselves of him! And no houseguest would convince their host to give them the boot, right? He will do everything in his power to convince his host that setting the den on fire was a good thing, a necessary thing—as was eating all the food in the fridge without replacing it, or flooding the bathroom.

Yes, it's true that each of these situations creates an opportunity for change (building a new den, purchasing fresh food, and cleaning the bathroom)—but change is already inevitable; everything is impermanent. What we are after is not the chaos of change but the fulfillment that comes from transformation. Don't let the Opponent confuse you!

Let's consider some examples of ways in which the Opponent persuades us to follow his will.

life rules

chapter six: never—and that means never—lay blame on other people or external events.

- You promised your father you would have dinner with him and his new wife, but a really important game came up at school (with the cheerleader you want to ask out leading the cheers). You want you to try out for the team next year, and you think it will impress the coach if you attend, so you cancel dinner at the last minute.

- Your best friend tells you her deepest, darkest secret and swears you to secrecy, to which you readily agree. But a few days later, after being unexpectedly included in a gossip session with the "in-crowd" girls, you find yourself divulging your friend's secret, unable to stop yourself, even though at that very moment you know it's wrong.

- You make a vow to finish your math homework by yourself for the rest of the semester, because you know that by doing it with your friend you are not really learning, just copying her results. But your friend offers to come by your house, and having her there does make everything easier. Not to mention, it frees up time for phone calls and chatting online.

- Your best friend is kicking his coke habit, and he needs you to spend the night with him so that he stays clean. You want to do the right thing by him, but there's a big party that night with some important people attending. And besides, you're not the one with a drug problem!

- One of your friends moves into the gigantic house on the hill—the one that you always used to daydream about living in—or shows up for English class in the very pair of boots you've been coveting for months. You try to tell yourself you are happy for her, and while part of you is, you can feel the jealousy bubbling. Resentment and happiness go to war for the control of your emotions.

You accidentally see one of the girls in your class throwing up in the bathroom. You sense that she does this after every meal. You know you should tell the teacher, but then everyone would think you're a tattletale and would give you a hard time.

This list could go on and on. We rarely respond to any situation with only one emotion. If we examine our responses honestly, we can inevitably find the thread that belongs to the Opponent and give it a good yank. Doing so will probably hurt, but that's only because he has convinced us that we are dependent upon him. But we're not!

When the Satan came into being, one of his first moves was to alter the DNA of the Desire to Receive. Before him, the Desire to Receive could be reconfigured into the Desire to Share. The Opponent changed this. The Desire to Receive became the Desire to Receive for the Self Alone. Like a black hole in deep space, this desire can consume everything within its vicinity so that even spiritual Light cannot escape its power!

We've all experienced this feeling—and most likely have felt lousy while doing so. If your friend shows up on a new titanium bike with 29-inch wheels and your heart jumps a bit because you want that bike for yourself, this is the Desire to Receive. In and of itself, this is not dangerous; it all depends on what you do with it. If, however, you buy the titanium bike first and then grow resentful of your neighbor for purchasing the same one, even though it in no way diminishes your own possession, this is the Desire to Receive for the Self Alone. This feeling makes for an exhausting way to live.

Do you remember the dessert I mentioned in the introduction to this book, and the feeling we have that if someone else takes some, then our portion will get smaller, or perhaps we won't get any at all? We've since learned that this simply isn't true. The

life rules

chapter six: never—and that means never—lay blame on other people or external events.

Opponent has attacked us and will continue to attack us on the level of our mind. Therefore, it's with our mind that we must fight back.

Take a moment now and point to the location of your mind. Most likely you have pointed to your head, to your brain. But are brain and mind the same thing? The brain is a physical organ that can be touched and dissected. Is the same true of the mind? Imagine a primitive tribesman venturing out of the jungle with no knowledge of the modern world. He comes across a transistor radio playing music and looks at it in astonishment, believing that the box is the source of the music. He opens up the radio and accidentally pulls out the battery. The music stops. He thinks he has killed a miraculous creature. Of course, we know that the source of the music is really a radio station broadcasting many miles away.

Our thoughts do not originate with the physical matter of the brain, just as the music did not originate from the physical matter of the radio. Instead, the brain is like an antenna, a receiving station that picks up a signal and then relays it to the conscious mind. And there are two cosmic broadcasters: the Light and the Satan. If only we could tell them apart, how much easier our lives would be!

Here are a few good starting points. If our thoughts seem logical and rational, and if the broadcast is loud and clear and urges us to react to a situation, then that is Satan. Any time we react, we are tuning in the Opponent. However, if the broadcast is faint and barely audible, perhaps emanating from some deep recess of our mind, then this is the Light. A sudden flash of intuition or inspiration, a potent dream, all originate in the 99% Realm.

The Opponent has nothing else to do but push our buttons—nothing else at all. He doesn't require sleep or food or use of the bathroom, so there are no times out. We must be prepared to

life rules

chapter six: never—and that means never—lay blame on other people or external events.

go to battle at a moment's notice. And the only way to fight him is by being proactive.

Now might be the time to introduce the Transformation Formula. We've discussed it in general terms, but now I'll give it to you in specific steps. This will teach you how to shut down the Satan's airwaves and let in more of the Light.

1. An obstacle occurs.

2. Realize that your reaction (the Opponent)—not the obstacle—is the real enemy and that the Opponent is, in fact, your ego.

3. Shut down your reactive system to allow the Light in.

4. Express your proactive nature. See yourself as the cause, as the creator, as a being of sharing.

The moment of transformation takes place during steps three and four. This is when you are able to plug into the 99% Realm, when you can touch the Light.

Let's see how these steps might look applied to a real-life situation. Let's say you run into your friend in the cafeteria, and she unexpectedly blows up at you. Fellow students are nearby, overhearing bits and pieces of her tirade. Although you don't even know what she's talking about, she is upsetting you. Now you're getting angry, and before you know it, you find yourself yelling right back at her. Sound familiar? As we've discussed, by yelling, you will most likely experience some level of exhilaration from reacting so spontaneously to your friend. You might experience a rush of feeling—not unlike a runner's high—that will quickly fade and leave you worn out, confused, and blue.

Let's apply the formula we just learned to this situation and see how things might play out if we tune in the Light and resist the Satan.

1.   An obstacle occurs. Your friend blows up at you in the lunchroom.

2.   Realize that your reaction is the real enemy. Your feelings of anger, hurt, and frustration are what you truly need to battle, not your friend.

3.   Shut down your reactive system to allow the Light in. Tap into that split-second pause before a decision is made. Let go of all your emotional reactions. Instead of shouting back, become an observer. Even if you're not to blame, let your friend vent. What matters isn't who is right or wrong. What matters is your decision not to react. Not reacting, however, is not the same as suppressing. We'll discuss this distinction further in Chapter Eight. But meanwhile, think of not reacting as taking responsibility for what is happening. If being hurt too easily and not trusting are issues that you need to overcome, then this fight is actually an opportunity to do so. Only by not reacting will you open yourself to that opportunity.

4.   Become the cause. Take responsibility for being part of this moment. Your friend is bringing up an issue you need to attend to; in this case it may be that you get hurt too readily and respond with anger, or that you're too caught up in what those around you might be thinking. Honor the gift your friend is bringing you. Then observe that the rest of this moment is about your friend. How can you do the best thing for her? Perhaps you could pull her aside and ask her calmly what's wrong.

life rules

chapter six: never—and that means never—lay blame on other people or external events.

You are now in contact with the 99% Realm. Your next set of actions will be rooted in the Light, which means that you will likely see a surprising positive change in the external situation that was confronting you. Your friend may well respond in a way that you never dreamed possible. Perhaps she'll tell you that her parents have been fighting a lot lately, or that she and her boyfriend are breaking up.

All day long, people and situations trigger reactions within us. Another student gets a higher grade. Your friend gets to go on vacation to the very place you wanted to go. The movie you want to see is sold out. Your parents can no longer afford the computer they promised you. Your favorite teacher picks on you in class. Your father walks out on your mom again. Now you know that these external circumstances are the Satan. And you know that you are not powerless before him. You have the power of the Light on your side. Draw strength from that.

When I was in junior high and high school, I didn't drink or do drugs, but certainly those around me did. Because of my ADD and my kabbalistic beliefs, not many kids were seeking me out to party, but opportunities did, on occasion, present themselves. Those situations were never easy. Believe me, during a great part of my school years, I wanted more than anything else to be cool, to be included. And what was cooler than doing drugs?

In junior high, it was usually pot that was passed my way, but in high school it was cocaine. The kids who were using these drugs claimed they made you feel as though you were God, made you unafraid of anything, made you feel at peace with yourself and the world. Plus, being cool might help me with girls. An enormous longing stirred within me. Drugs and alcohol seemed like a logical palliative to the pain of loneliness. Their benefits sounded a lot like the 99% Realm, so my curiosity was piqued. Fortunately I remembered that the Satan speaks with terrific logic! And just as luckily, my parents had raised me to respect my intuition,

life rules

chapter six: never—and that means never—lay blame on other people or external events.

which told me that nothing from the Endless could be reduced down to the size of a pill.

Although I was lucky enough not to succumb, I did need to apply the Transformation Formula in order to resist the allure of drugs. My obstacle was the kid in front of me offering me not only drugs, but popularity and freedom from suffering! This was quite a temptation. My reaction was desire. I could easily have accepted the drugs, but I found that moment in time before a choice is made and resisted my craving. And rather than make up excuses or engage in any behavior that would hurt my class-mate or myself, I simply shook my head and walked away.

Believe me, this didn't do much for my popularity. I was once more the outcast. But in that moment of Resistance—in that moment when I recognized that my craving was simply the Opponent—I plugged in to the 99% Realm. And once you expe-rience *that* kind of high, you can't be bothered with anything less. You just want to figure out how to make the real thing last.

This chapter is about doing battle. And the first step in that bat-tle is accepting responsibility for every single one of our thoughts, words, and actions. As long as we blame others, Satan is pleased. In fact, he's not only pleased, he's rejuvenated. And a rejuvenated Satan is one that will throw you so many obstacles that you may feel you are being unfairly singled out. Stop nurturing him. Resist. Practice the Transformation Formula as much as possible. Use it when you can't get the skateboard you want. Use it when the kid next door to you does. Use it when your mother is mad at you. Use it when you are mad at your mother. You can read this book a million times, but if you don't practice what you are reading, the words will remain merely words. And the Satan will grow stronger.

You can't go into battle if you don't first go into training. If you skip the training, your chances of being injured, or dying, go way, way up. You will most likely be injured, and perhaps even die. So think of this book—and your journal—as boot camp. You are training your mind to engage in the most important battle of your life: the battle to overcome the Satan.

○   We are responsible for our thoughts, words, and actions.

○   If something else is always to blame, then it is the cause and we are merely the effect, in which case we have no power to change the situation.

○   In order to rid ourselves of Bread of Shame, we need an Opponent. This is the Satan, which is our ego or our reactive behavior.

○   The voice of the Satan comes to us as logical, rational, and loud. It urges us to react.

The voice of the Light is intuitive, inspirational, and non invasive, often coming to us in dreams. It encourages us to respond proactively.

Transformation Formula:
1. An obstacle occurs.
2. Realize that your reaction (the Opponent) is the enemy and that the Opponent is, in fact, your ego.
3. Shut down your reactive system to allow the Light in.
4. Express your proactive nature.

We are able to plug into the 99% Realm between steps three and four, which is the moment of transformation.

One of the key things we need to learn is how to distinguish the voice of the Light from the voice of the Satan. Let's begin with the Light. Write down the last dream you had in as much detail as you can remember. Without getting caught up in interpreting the dream, simply read through everything you wrote. Then read it again. Recognize that these images are part of the 99% Realm. It's okay if you don't understand them right now. All you are trying to do is to train your mind to accept dreams as a potent aspect of the Light. The more you open up to them, the more you respect them, the more sense your dreams will start to make.

Now write down the last time you had a gut feeling about something, however faintly—a feeling that let you know that something you were about to do was beneficial or harmful. Go into as much detail as possible. How did your body register your intuition? How did your mind register it? Did you act on that hunch? And if so, what happened? If not, what happened, and what might have happened if you had? As always, you are not looking to judge yourself. By writing down your intuitive experiences, you are opening yourself to having more of them, to understand them more clearly, and to allow them to draw you closer to the Light.

Now let's check out the Satan's voice. Write down the last time you were swayed by an external event. Don't overthink this. If you are human, you are swayed by the Opponent all the time. Connecting with the Light's voice may require paying special attention, but the Satan's voice is loud and constant. Write down what form your obstacle took. Be sure to make note of your emotional reaction as well as your behavior. How did you feel when this interaction was complete?

Now rewrite the scenario, but this time apply the Transformation Formula. Your obstacle will remain the same, as will your emotional reaction. But imagine a scenario in which you shut down your reactive system to allow in the Light, and then express your proactive nature. Don't just imagine this in your head. Get it down on paper. Try this with two or three more examples. By allowing yourself to respond differently on the page, you are also training yourself to respond differently in real life. Remember, you can't go into battle if you don't first practice your maneuvers at boot camp. So be diligent. Put the blame where it belongs. And prepare to fight!

resist your reactive impulses, knowing that this is the way to create lasting light.

7

7

O ne of the Satan's most potent weapons is time. Time is an illusion. It doesn't exist in the 99% Realm, and it had no place before the Vessel resisted, before the curtains dropped. In the 1% Realm in which we live, time creates the distance between cause and effect, between action and reaction. It's the space between activity and repercussion, the divide between crime and consequence.

Without the illusion of time, past, present, and future would fold into one unified whole. This is the way of the 99% Realm. There we have no trouble detecting cause and effect. Chaos melts away.

I know this notion of unified time seems inconceivable. In fact, however, only the limits of our consciousness keep us from seeing yesterday and tomorrow right now!

Imagine a 30-story building. You are standing on the 15th floor, which represents the present moment. Floors 1 through 14 represent the past. Floors 16 through 30 represent your future. What do you perceive right now, with your five senses? Only the 15th floor. You cannot see the floors below or the floors above. Therefore your logical mind (remember to whom logic belongs) convinces you that the 15th floor is all that can exist. But the truth is that all the floors—past, present, and future—exist equally as part of one building. If you could float outside the building's 15th floor, you would see all 30 stories at once! What a lesson that would be!

Time is the source of much of our suffering. The past haunts us, filling us with sadness or regret. We wish we could relive it in order to fix things or simply to enjoy them all over again. Viewing time as something that passes can make the present seem unbearable. While we acknowledge that this is the only moment we live in, we seldom allow our minds to rest here. Instead, we constantly revisit our past or anticipate our future. In some

life rules

chapter seven: resist your reactive impulses, knowing that this is the way to create lasting light.

sense, we are thereby creating a unified whole—but this one is based on fear rather than joy, and it is not lasting.

The future terrifies many of us. We see it as our way out of our less-than-satisfactory present, yet we are also uncertain if it will play out the way we desire. The future is constantly here, and yet we are unable to truly connect with it. In the time it took you to read the previous paragraph, for example, your future became your present and then became your past again. But do you feel any different? Has your life become better? Or worse? If we could embrace the notion of concurrent existence, we might find that many of our demands and expectations would melt away— and with them, much of our suffering.

When I was in high school, one of my parents' friends was diagnosed with cancer, and the doctors offered little hope. Naturally, for the woman, the first few weeks of living with this news was very painful. Sometimes she seemed very angry, and at other times terribly sad. But not long afterward, I remember talking to this woman and was surprised to find her quite happy. She told me that she'd never felt more alive, that she rarely allowed thoughts of the past or the future to distract her from whatever was in front of her in that very moment. Because every moment felt precious to her, all the people in her life became especially precious as well.

This is not an unusual story. When people are faced with death, they often become hyperaware of their present. My parents' friend confided in me that she felt her cancer was the greatest gift she'd ever received. It made her acutely aware that time was something we all too often used to avoid being fully in the present.

The work you are doing with this book isn't easy. You are facing your fears and are seeking the courage to transform those fears into the Light. This is big stuff. You may already have experienced moments in which your mind became tired or became overly active with other thoughts. As you drew close to some truths, you may have felt the urge to go to sleep, or perhaps found yourself mentally reliving a conversation with a friend or planning how you're going to get enough money to buy something you want. This is the Opponent at work, drawing you into the past and keeping you there, spinning over what you said, she said, he said—or tricking you into dwelling on the future, envisioning how much better your life would be if only you had this or that. In every scenario, he's dangling a carrot—and time after time, we go after it.

We are all going to die. It's easy enough to forget this, especially when we are young. And certainly your friends may consider you morbid if you spend too much time thinking about it! But I was struck by how serene my parents' friend became when she realized that her days were limited. All of our days are limited, and rarely do we know just how much time we have. My parents' friend actually went on to live for several more years, and while she had her ups and downs, she never lost the rich appreciation of life that her acceptance of death had given her.

Experiment with training your mind to stay in this moment. This one, right now. Don't dodge it. Don't overthink it. Just experience it. Consider how your body feels. The temperature in the room. The surface you're sitting on. The noise from the street. Observe your thoughts without judging them. You are learning simply how to be with yourself.

This is an invaluable tool for transformation. The Satan does not want us to be with ourselves. He wants our minds to be scattered along the past, the present, and the future—a time line that extends like dirty clothes strewn across your bedroom floor. This way we won't be in fighting condition. So to thwart him, we need to ground ourselves. Start now. Start here. If your mind wanders, let it go. But recognize what it is doing. Be aware that

life rules

chapter seven: resist your reactive impulses, knowing that this is the way to create lasting light.

this is the Opponent distracting you from your true path. Consider that time is merely a weapon in his extensive arsenal.

Not only does the Opponent use time as a means to distract us from the all-important present, but he also uses its delaying quality to support the idea that bad deeds go unpunished and good deeds go unrewarded. The neighbor who molested your friend's little sister walks away on a technicality while your aunt's car, which she uses to deliver food to people with AIDS, is stolen after she canceled her insurance for lack of funds. Because of this delay, we also have difficulty perceiving the interconnectedness of all things. Ten or fifteen years ago we might have planted a negative seed with a harsh word or an act of cruelty, but by the time the seed sprouts, we've forgotten all about it. Eventually, something unpleasant will "suddenly" appear out of nowhere. Yet as we now know, everything has a reason; there is always a cause. Chaos appears to be sudden because time has separated cause and effect. It may be that the rapist of whom we spoke had planted a good seed long before he embarked on his current destructive course—perhaps even in another lifetime. It simply came into fruition during his court case, making it appear as though he just got lucky. (At some point, we must all face the consequences of our actions - large or small, good or bad. It might take days, weeks, months, decades, or even lifetimes, but repercussions are inevitable.)

In this way, the Satan uses time to foster doubt. If we see someone engage in a cruel act and seem to get away with it, this may make us wonder if there is any merit in this Kabbalah stuff after all. What kind of spiritual or social system allows bad guys such as the rapist to go unpunished? One thing to keep in mind is that it is impossible to know if you are seeing a good or a bad seed coming to fruition. When the rapist is released from prison, for example, it may look like a good development as he strolls scot-free back to his home. Yet if, when he gets there, the father of the little girl he raped stabs him repeatedly and leaves him to slowly bleed to death on the sidewalk, his release may not look like such a fortunate turn of events after all.

The Opponent also challenges our faith by delaying access to the Light. If we have resisted a reaction but the Light does not shine immediately, we may feel ripped off, or perhaps we may doubt the authenticity of these teachings. In the example of your aunt whose car was stolen, you may feel outrage. Where are the fruits of her good deeds? But had your aunt driven the car on the following day, she might have been in a terrible accident, or the car might have broken down and stranded her somewhere unsafe. If we react to the Satan's delay, we will begin to doubt what we know to be true. Because time separates cause from effect, it creates a convincing illusion of space. If you cheat on a test in math class, the chaos may show up in your social life rather than in your studies. If you lie to your mother, the effect may be seen in your diminished athletic performance. You may abuse your classmates all through your high school years and no one may ever be cruel to you in return. But this doesn't mean you have eluded the effect of your bad actions. Instead, they may manifest 20 years from now, when you are living on another continent, in the form of a stock market crash in which you lose your entire fortune. Conversely, volunteering at the local animal shelter doesn't mean that animals will forever be kind to you. Perhaps they will be, or perhaps you are planting a good seed that will ripen that summer in the form of the best vacation you've ever had.

When the Light we generate through proactive behavior at school materializes at home, the Satan will distract us so much so that we don't even notice how well we are suddenly getting along with our parents. When the Light does not materialize as a date to the prom or as election to the student council, we assume that our proactive behavior is not working. The Opponent limits our view and focuses our attention on situations that fuel our ego.

life rules

chapter seven: resist your reactive impulses, knowing that this is the way to create lasting light.

The Satan's greatest strength lies in his power to confuse us. He makes us forget that he is the Opponent. He convinces us that our friends, our family, our neighbors are the Opponent. Or our teacher. Or the kid who just moved in next door. Or the girl who made fun of our new coat. Or the boy who asked us out when we weren't sure we wanted him to. When things aren't going as you'd hoped they would, this is the time to remember not to blame other people or events. Instead, the next time you feel as if you've been wronged, imagine the Opponent standing right in front of you, whispering his script into your tormentor's ear! See that person falling under the sway of the masterful Opponent. And imagine the Opponent laughing and growing stronger at the chaos he is unleashing. He is having the time of his life, no doubt about it! The only way to wreck his party is to not react. Remember the three R's: Resistance, Resistance, and Resistance!

When kabbalists speak of Light with a capital "L," they are referring to the infinite Light of the Creator. When they speak of light with a lowercase "l," they are referring to conventional light such as sunlight or the light of a bulb. Yet both Light and light share the property of providing illumination. A light bulb generates light using three components: a positive pole (+), a negative pole (-), and a filament separating the (+) from the (-). Within the bulb, the filament actually plays the most important role: It acts as a resistor, pushing back the current flowing from the positive and preventing it from connecting directly with the negative. This resistance, or pushing back of energy, is the reason the bulb turns on. Now think of the Vessel as the negative pole, the Light as the positive, and the filament as the Vessel's act of Resistance. By consistently resisting, the Vessel has tapped into its greatest source of fulfillment: being the creator of its own Light!

This is exactly what we are seeking to do. By consistently resisting, we will be able to maintain lasting Light. And not just glimmers here and there (we all know how frustrating it is when a light bulb is on the blink), but steady Light. This Light is not dependent on time or space. Nor is it dependent on the Opponent.

○ Past, present, and future exist simultaneously.

○ The Satan uses our belief that time is divided to distract us from the present moment. He does so by using time as a means of delaying consequences and fostering doubt. He uses space in the same manner.

○ The Satan's greatest tool is his ability to confuse us. He makes us forget that our reactive behavior is the Opponent and convinces us that it's our friend, parent, or neighbor.

Cause and effect are inevitable. Every action, good or bad, plants a seed. Every seed will ripen. It may take seconds, days, years, or life-times, but it will ripen.

In a light bulb, it is the ongoing resistance of the filament between positive and negative poles that creates the light. In the same way, by consistently resisting our reactive behavior, we will have continuous access to the Light.

Most likely you have been experimenting with resisting your reactive behavior. This is wonderful. Take the time now to list some recent examples, being as specific as you can. In some cases your efforts will have brought you your desired results, and in others your behavior will still be reactive despite your best efforts. Don't worry. This is tricky stuff. After listing your recent moments of Resistance, go ahead and make a note of how you felt during and after each scenario. Consider how your body felt, as well as your mind and your psyche. Take a moment now and compare these notes with those from Chapter Five. Look for places of overlap, and look for places of growth. Can you see concrete ways in which resisting has already improved your life? Make note of these. Imagine stringing enough of these together, like a necklace of pearls, so that you are never separated from the Light! This is our goal.

reactive behavior creates intense sparks of light but eventually leaves darkness in its wake.

8

life rules

chapter eight: reactive behavior creates intense sparks of light but eventually leaves darkness in its wake.

Nestled within our reactive behavior is the desire for instant gratification. It offers a quick high that makes us feel alive and in control of our lives. We can become addicted to this feeling, just as a runner does to endorphins or a drug addict to heroin, crack, or cocaine.

As we saw in the case of our light bulb, when we resist reactive behavior, we generate Light. When we opt instead for instant gratification, we also create a very bright light. A direct connection occurs between our reactive desire (the negative pole) and the Light (the positive pole), producing a momentary flash of delight followed by darkness, because the bulb has burned itself out. This is one of the unseen laws of the universe, not unlike gravity. If you jump out of a tall building, you will fall to the street below even if you are unaware of the existence of gravity. The same holds true of electricity. If you play with a live, high-voltage wire, you will get electrocuted even if you can't see the source of your demise

If you connect directly with the Light without the careful use of Restriction (the decision not to have immediate gratification), you will reenact what happened in the Endless when the Light fed the Vessel (without fulfillment) and created Bread of Shame. If you satisfy your desire right away without first becoming the cause of your life, the experience will burn you out. But that immediate delight can be so seductive that we find ourselves engaging in the same behavior again and again.

One of the reasons I didn't do drugs in high school—or mess around with alcohol, or even smoke cigarettes—was that I knew where such behavior would take me. A lot of folks who have come to The Centre had once been drug addicts or were still struggling to clean up. These people had lost huge chunks of their lives. So much time and energy that could have been devoted to development and personal progress had been expended on trying to re-create a transitory moment of pleasure.

life rules

chapter eight: reactive behavior creates intense sparks of light but eventually leaves darkness in its wake.

I remember spending one afternoon chatting with a man in his mid-30s who had done Ecstasy since he was in his teens. Although he was clean now, it wasn't easy for him to stay off drugs. Every morning he had to recommit to steering his life in a new and better direction. He had to recommit himself to resisting Ecstasy, to resisting the temporary pleasure it gave him. He explained to me that the first time he had taken the drug, he had experienced a high unlike any other he had ever known, and he had spent the bulk of his life trying not only to find that high again but to make it last longer.

Drug addicts put themselves through an inordinate amount of pain and suffering. They lose both self-respect and respect for others. Every time they snort, shoot, lick, or swallow, they skip over Resistance to touch the Light directly. And because of that, they burn themselves out. Many are aware of this, but they still can't stop. Sadly, they spend the rest of their lives in reactive behavior. They have become the effect of the drug, allowing the drug to be the cause, the creator of their day-to-day lives.

Much like junkies, we become addicted to our reactive behaviors. We put ourselves through an inordinate amount of pain and suffering by dashing after that transient high, whether it's a compliment on our cool new jeans or the kick we get from winning that computer game. And just as this man had to recommit each morning to staying clean, we must recommit to Resistance as the best path to revealing the Light. In the beginning, we will fail as often as not. But even if this happens thousands of times— which it probably will—just keep getting back on the horse. Remember, every time you assert your conscious intent to resist, you reveal more of the Light.

We can also become addicted to people and to relationships. Think of how many times you have felt you couldn't live without a particular friend, or family member, or someone you were dating. Perhaps you couldn't stop smiling when you saw a boyfriend, and it didn't matter what you talked about so long as you were both in the same room. Certain songs, or a particular smell or type of clothing, would make you think of him when you were apart. And your heart probably raced at the thought of losing him, of having to give him up. And haven't you had times when it seemed impossible to get through a situation without a sister or a best friend? You needed them in order to feel capable and complete.

All of this—even the pleasurable part—is addictive behavior. In it, our self-worth becomes entangled in what *they* think of us, how *they* see us, how we feel when we are with *them*. We've made the other person the cause and left ourselves to be the effect. Before long, we are searching everywhere for that exchange of energy, that high, until—boom!—it explodes in our face. Once more, we've touched the Light directly.

Addiction is not to be confused with affection. Having affection for someone—wishing that person happiness, or wishing them to be free from suffering—is a wonderful thing. This is what we are striving for: unlimited love and compassion. With affection, we do not feel as if our very existence is tangled up with another's. Addiction, on the other hand, is like glue. We feel useless without that special person. We can feel as if there is no point to our lives without them. We may feel as if they also need us to fix them. Yet we are probably addicted not only to holding hands and sharing frappucinos, but also to the fights and the misunderstandings and the drama. Drama is a reactive behavior. Many people mistake it as proof of passion, proof of love. But it is merely another form of instant gratification. It is simply the Opponent at play.

Kabbalah offers one way to strip away our self-deceptions, to encourage spending time with ourselves and with our minds. If we are continually reacting to people and events, our mind is constantly churning, and we do not allow ourselves the

life rules

chapter eight: reactive behavior creates intense sparks of light but eventually leaves darkness in its wake.

opportunity to explore it, to befriend it, to tame it. This leads to dissatisfaction and perhaps to anxiety or depression. Depression is a direct result of spending too much time thinking of ourselves. If we can remember that our purpose in this life is to return to the Light, then we can transform the relationship from "What am I getting?" into "What can I give to him or her? What do I have to offer the world?"

I remember all-too-rare invitations to high school parties. These were awkward moments for me, since no one at these parties truly felt like my friend. Nevertheless, I enjoyed the moments when one of my classmates might tell a joke and we would all laugh, or when a few kids would came over and spend five or ten minutes shooting the breeze with me. I remember how happy I was. I felt acknowledged and appreciated. During those moments, I felt included and even, in a small way, important. But as soon as the party was over, all the high from those interactions evaporated, and my feelings of importance and value went along with it. By the time I returned home, I was often quite blue.

What I came to realize was that during these parties, I was in reactive mode. I was happy because people were turning their attention toward me, not because of anything I was generating. Since my happiness was dependent on an outside source, however, it was to be expected that when I separated from that source, I was going to feel a loss of the Light. This is the same feeling the drug addict from The Centre went through when he ran out of Ecstasy. He would fall into a deep depression, a darkness, and the only way he knew to access the Light was to find more "e." I could be cheered up again by more interactions with the kids from my school—but since I was merely reacting to their behavior, no matter how positive those interactions might have been, the happiness wouldn't last. Eventually I grew tired of living with my mood swings and set about generating my own happiness.

This is not to say that interactions with others are useless. Quite the opposite; they are vital and necessary. But to rely on them or on anything other than yourself to generate the Light is futile. If you pop a pill, the effects of that pill will eventually wear off, and you will be left with yourself. If you fall madly in love, over time the relationship will change and perhaps end, and you will be left with yourself. If you gamble your belongings away, you will get swept up in a rush of adrenaline—but that too will fade, and you will be left with yourself. If you engage in endless one-night stands, at some point your body will need rest and you will be left with yourself. No matter what you do to take yourself away from your present moment, eventually it will end. Everything is impermanent. Nothing can last forever. And when it ends, you will be left with yourself and the reality of life you have chosen. Friends, family, and even enemies can all help us navigate our lives, but when we expect them to be the source of our own Light, we run into trouble. Fighting or making love with them may provide us with momentary glimpses of the Light, but if we want anything lasting, we must practice Resistance.

Examples of revealing the Light through Resistance can be found in every area of our lives. When we listen to a violinist play an instrument, sound waves are created by the resistance of the bow against the strings. We experience the music when our eardrums resist the sound. We've all seen those breathtaking images of the earth from space: Like a sparkling blue jewel, the earth radiates gloriously against the velvety blackness. Once again, the principle of Resistance is responsible. The earth's atmosphere resists the sun's light, creating illumination. But the void of space produces no Resistance whatsoever, so what we see in the background is darkness.

We humans possess the free will necessary to resist pleasurable energy generated by reactive impulses. However, the exercise of free will requires the need to make a choice, and in this case we are faced with all the powers of the Opponent as he tries to persuade us not to resist. Isn't it better, the Opponent might argue, to have some pleasure—few and far between as those moments may be—than to have none at all? Sure. But not if the fleeting moments come at the expense of eternal Light. Go back and consider the example of our light bulb. Right before the bulb blows, it gives off the brightest light of its life—but by doing so, it loses its steady light. Lack of Resistance generates quite an impressive flare-up, but it is followed by utter darkness. What use is a burned-out light bulb when we want to read in bed at night, or if we need to stay up late doing homework, or if a younger sibling is afraid of the dark? When you earn some money for mowing the lawn or cleaning the kitchen, you can choose to blow it right away on video games and candy, or you can save it up for something bigger that adds to the quality of your life. In exactly the same way, you can choose how you would like to access the Light. I would like to encourage you to think about the long term, to think about the Light that always burns.

○ Instant gratification—filling your desire without applying Resistance —results in a direct connection between you and the Light. This produces an immense spark, but one that immediately fades.

○ It is easy to become addicted to this momentary flash. These addictions can take many forms, including drugs, alcohol, ciga-rettes, love, sex, food, and gam-bling.

○ During instant gratification, we reenact the Endless. Whatever we are addicted to becomes the cause, and we become the effect.

A burned-out light bulb doesn't do anyone any good. In this same way, flashes of intense light will provide only brief glimmers. If you want to steadily illuminate your path, you need to apply Resistance.

We all struggle with the desire to resist, but this struggle requires a lot of discipline and faith. So don't be ashamed of the times you forget to resist—or simply don't want to resist. Instead, make note of them. As long as you are raising your awareness around your own behavior, your actions will begin to change. Take the time now to write about some recent encounters in which you've felt high from reactive behavior. These can be "good" times or frustrating times. Make a note of staying up late with friends or lazy days in the park, as well as rip-roaring fights with a girlfriend or parent. Describe how the high felt. Be specific. How long did the sparks last? Seconds, minutes, hours, perhaps days? How did you feel after they were gone? Better or worse than before?

obstacles are our opportunity to connect to the light.

9

9

life rules

chapter nine: obstacles are our opportunity to connect to the light.

This is an important step, in part because it's counterintuitive. We go through our lives primarily trying to *do away* with obstacles. Whether we're exercising, meditating, getting drunk, falling head over heels in love, beating up a rival, throwing up our meals, or simply not eating those meals, we are all trying to create an obstacle-free life. Because without obstacles, we can finally be happy, right?

This step provides you with a whole new way to view obstacles. Although supplied by the Satan, obstacles are gifts nonetheless, because only by applying Resistance can we access the Light. And without obstacles, we have nothing to resist. So the next time you are confronted by a problem, rather than immediately becoming anxious or angry or overwhelmed or panicked, find that moment before your decision to react is made and look at what's going on. Good, bad, or indifferent, these judgments are secondary to the act of observation itself. Just let yourself be with your response. Don't judge it; simply experience it.

Remember the two realms. We spend most of our time in the 1% Realm, which is rife with chaos and uncertainty, but there is a vast and rewarding 99% Realm that we are learning to tap into. The things that we really want—lasting love, peace, harmony, security, true power, well-being—are things that do not exist in the physical realm. They exist only in the 99%. Therefore, to achieve this lasting fulfillment, we need to connect to the 99% Realm in a consistent manner.

This is the beauty of obstacles. An obstacle is the Light coming in, just not directly. Because of this, we can safely interact with it without fear of explosions or burnout. Oftentimes, right behind our biggest obstacles can be found the biggest opening to the Light. We have all heard the saying, "The calm before the storm," but obstacles are our storms before the calm. Without fixing our problems ourselves, we can never become the cause. Therefore, obstacles are blessings! They provide us with countless opportunities to draw closer to the Light.

life rules

chapter nine: obstacles are our opportunity to connect to the light.

Without a doubt, viewing obstacles as your new friend is going to take some getting used to. There may be many, many times when you shut down to this notion. Kabbalah is an invitation to notice your limits and not get carried away by the hopes and fears that surround them. If you shut down to this process at various times, that's fine. You will begin to clearly see that you are shutting down or running away. And you will no longer be able to do so in ignorance. That in itself begins to cast light, since ignorance is a choice of ego, and ego is the curtain. Bear in mind that if you shut down and run away from your obstacle, you are actually running away from the very Light you so naturally long for.

Many of us want what we want exactly when we want it—forget obstacles. But we might not always be prepared to handle what we think we want. One of the kids I went to school with was super-rich. Right before he turned 16, he drove his parents nuts begging them for a Porsche. And he drove all of *us* nuts telling us that he was going to get a Porsche—even though he hadn't even taken a driver's ed course yet! I remember my brother saying to me, "If his parents give him that car, it will be his death sentence." Fortunately, the boy's parents disappointed him on his birthday. What they did do was enroll him in a driving class— and then, when he had his permit, they took him out of the city on weekends and let him drive their big Cadillac on the highway.

Many months later, after he had earned his driver's license, the boy's parents still didn't buy him the Porsche—although they could have afforded to give him one in each color. Instead they bought him an old Volvo, which was safe and reliable. They let him get used to caring for his own car and waited for him to learn to drive responsibly and with confidence. I heard through the grapevine that when the boy finally graduated from college, his folks finally gave him the Porsche. By that time, he had dealt with many obstacles and could thus enjoy the car's power and speed without risking his own safety, or the safety of others.

These were smart parents. Even back then, I knew they were doing the right thing. The Creator does the same thing with us. For instance, we may want a soul mate more than anything else. And we may think it's very unfair that we haven't met him or her yet. But we may be too young or too immature to really nurture and develop such a profound relationship. So instead, the Light sends us a relationship that is full of obstacles—obstacles that, if we understand them as opportunities, will help us develop into a person who is truly ready for a soul mate. The purpose of the obstacles is to give us a chance to earn the very thing that we so intensely desire.

Each of us has our limits. This obstacle here we can embrace, this obstacle there we can shake hands with—but this next obstacle we must run from full tilt. For one friend of mine, getting on an airplane is her limit. For my uncle, it's having to cook meals for more than, say, four people. For someone else, it may be confronting a friend who has been peeking at her answers during a quiz. What produces fear or hope in me is not what produces it in you. Recognizing your limits will help you break through them. It will also help you address them with kindness, diligence, and humor.

When people begin to practice the steps in this book, certain pitfalls always show up. One of them involves confusing resistance with suppression. The difference here is that suppression has nothing to do with viewing your reactive behavior honestly. In fact, suppression means not viewing your behavior at all, but stuffing it somewhere deep and far away instead. At first glance these responses may look the same, but in the long run they are anything but.

In junior high, there was a boy in my science class who constantly copied answers off my tests and in-class assignments. I could sense him staring over my shoulder and could feel his breath on my back, and this irritated me beyond words. I felt he

life rules

chapter nine: obstacles are our opportunity to connect to the light.

was taking advantage of me. He was one of the popular boys, and while I was at home studying, he was out having fun. I didn't feel he should be able to have fun and do well in class because of my efforts, so his actions outraged me. They triggered my reactive behavior!

I had begun to study Kabbalah with my father by that time, so I already knew that by reacting, I was only going to make things worse. So rather than confront this boy, I pushed my feelings down deep. I honestly thought I was applying the Transformation Formula—but instead of feeling any sense of relief, let alone the Light, things grew worse and worse. My irritation festered, and soon I grew to hate this boy. Ironically, he was one of the kids who would talk to me at parties and nod to me in the hall—but these moments of kindness only fueled my hatred, which grew in leaps and bounds.

Finally, when I couldn't take it anymore, I exploded at the boy one day during class. He was straining so hard to copy my answers on a midterm that his head was practically on my shoulder. I turned to him and shouted, *Stop copying from me! Stop taking everything from me!* He was, quite naturally, shocked—as was the rest of the class, not to mention the teacher. It was one of the most embarrassing moments of my life, but also one of my greatest lessons. I had confused suppression with resistance, with explosive results. Had I resisted my reactive behavior, I might have chosen to talk to this boy outside of school one day, or in the lunchroom during a calmer moment—a moment in which I was not in the thick of my reactive emotions. I might even have discovered, as I later did, that the boy wasn't out carousing every night. In fact, his grandfather was quite ill, and the family had brought him to their house to die. Much of the boy's time after school was wrapped up in caring for his grandfather. Finding time to study had thus become a luxury.

life rules

chapter nine: obstacles are our opportunity to connect to the light.

We must be careful not to confuse taming our reactions with being a doormat. If I felt that this kid's copying of my work was problematic for me, then chances are it was. And there would have been nothing wrong with trying to remedy the situation. According to Kabbalah, everything happens for a reason. In this instance, it might have been an opportunity for me to speak with this kid in a caring manner. By doing so, I might have discovered ways I could help—and by helping, even more Light would have been available to me. Plus, it might have led to an amazing friendship. Instead, I picked myself up off the floor of shame, and set about being the cause with clearer understanding. What we are learning to work with is the energy we bring to our responses. Obstacles will always be with us. That is something we cannot change. But what we can change is how we greet them.

Another pitfall involves confusing coping with resisting. Coping is certainly an improvement over suppressing. When you are coping with something, at least you have acknowledged the situation and your emotions. You have identified your limits within that situation and are trying to work with them. These are all positive steps.

But coping rarely leads to change. Only by applying Resistance with the intention of removing Bread of Shame can we begin to uproot the seed of the problem.

One of the guys at my junior high, Jimmy, had a younger sister who was bulimic, only we didn't truly understand that at the time. All we knew was that she was really pretty and really, really thin. Jimmy's mother walked her two kids to school each morning, dropping Jimmy off at our school first and then taking his sister to her school, which was a couple of blocks away. Julia seemed thinner every time we saw her, and summer was always startling to us because she didn't wear her big parka, so we could all see how fragile she really was. She never looked any of us in the eye, and she rarely smiled, though her face lit up when she did.

life rules

chapter nine: obstacles are our opportunity to connect to the light.

Sometimes when we went on school field trips, we would partner up with Julia's school. Then we'd share buses, wander down museum halls together, and eat side by side in the lunchrooms. One time Julia finished her meal and got up to use the bathroom. As she did, I heard some of the girls say, "Oh, she's just going to throw it up again. I don't know why she bothers eating in the first place."

When I saw Julia again, she'd put on a bit of weight. I heard that her parents had put her in behavioral therapy, and that the doctors had put her on some medication. Now when she stood by her mother's side, she could look us in the eye more often, and during school trips she could talk to us with much greater ease. It was during one of these trips that Julia first met my mother, who was a volunteer chaperone. Perhaps because she had been through so much in her life, Julia was much more open to the teachings of Kabbalah than were other kids her age. As she confided to my mother, she was able to cope, but she didn't feel truly alive.

Soon Julia began coming around to The Centre regularly, sometimes joining us at home for dinner. The ideas of Kabbalah made a lot of sense to her, and she worked hard to bring them into her life. Initially it took a lot of willpower for her to share meals with us, and even more not to dash to the bathroom afterward—but after a while she relaxed. We watched her face fill out, and then her body. Her breathing opened up, and her color improved. By the time she began high school, Julia was off her medications and doing volunteer work with other people who were struggling with eating disorders. She told my mother that she had completely rid herself of the feelings that formed the basis of her low self-esteem. Rather than just coping with her situation, Julia had gone to the roots and dug up the seed.

If you are having a chronic problem with bees, let's say, it makes sense to put screens on your windows. This is a coping technique. The bees still exist, but other than the very persistent one or two that make it past your screens, they no longer bother you. But should a screen rip apart or be left open, the bees will be right back in your home. You thus have to stay diligent about those screens at all times, and that can be exhausting. But if, after installing the screens, you go outside and determine that you have a beehive, then you have an opportunity to remove the beehive and correct the situation at its core.

Spiritual transformation does not mean seeking refuge from life's problems. It's not about lighting candles and thinking only happy thoughts. It's about facing the chaos of life and our reactions to it head on. If we are sitting on a pillow somewhere serene with our eyes closed, we might feel temporarily refreshed, but we're not going to uproot any of the behaviors or patterns in our lives that continually bring us pain. Open your eyes! See the obstacles! Be grateful that they exist! Overcome them one by one! And let the Light shine!

○ Obstacles come from the Satan—our egos. They are gifts in that they allow us to apply Resistance and access the Light.

○ Obstacles are the Light coming to us indirectly so that we can access it without burning out.

○ Obstacles help us grow and develop so that we will be able to receive our true desires.

○ Suppression is not Resistance. If you push your reactions down deep, you will explode at some point.

While better than suppression, coping is not the right tool for uprooting the problems posed by your ego. Only Resistance can offer this.

Consider the last fight or disagreement you had with a friend or family member. Write down what you fought about. Did what they wanted feel like an obstacle to you? Were their desires blocking yours in some way? How did you respond to facing that obstacle? How did you handle your emotions around it? Did you suppress your emotions? Pretend they weren't happening? Did you let the person take advantage of you in some way, thinking that resisting your reactive behavior meant no longer having responses to anything? Did you cope with your emotions? Did you figure out useful ways to recognize your emotions and let them exist without uprooting them? Or did you respond even more proactively? Did you recognize your reactive behavior and find a way to express your desires without falling back into your old patterns? How did you feel about your response? What are some ways you might change your response should a similar situation arise in the future?

the greater the obstacle, the greater the potential light.

10

10

A t least once a week during lunch hour, I went to the deli right across the street from my high school. Although my mother would always have packed me something, I often had a craving for a bagel. They were brought in fresh twice a day, and our school break corresponded with the second delivery. My favorite was the onion bagel with a thin layer of cream cheese. I had been going to this deli for so long that the counter guys there all knew me and would cut and toast my bagel before I'd even make it from the door to the counter. I felt very honored by this. It gave me the sense of belonging that I longed for in those days.

There was only one guy—an older man, with thick, graying side-burns and bushy eyebrows—who made me place my order every time. While the other counter guys might ask me how my studies were going or, as I grew older, if I'd met a nice girl, this man never spoke to me about anything personal. I'd request an onion bagel, please, with just a smidgen of cream cheese. And when it was ready, he wouldn't hand it to me directly as the others did; he would leave it with the cashier. Then, when I opened my bagel, it would invariably be thick with cream cheese, most of which I'd have to scrape off before I could eat it.

At first I would scrape the cream cheese off outside the deli, because I didn't want the man to feel bad about having made a mistake. But as time went on and he continually ignored my request for just a dab of cream cheese, I began to scrape it off right in front of him, hoping he'd get the message. I never con-fronted him directly. I thought I'd teach him a lesson in humility by conspicuously removing the excess cream cheese. But if the man noticed, he certainly never let on.

Just as I had taken personally the other men remembering my standing order, I also took personally the fact that this man con-sistently messed up my order. As I cleaned off my bagel, I observed his interactions with other customers. Sometimes he

life rules

chapter ten: the greater the obstacle, the greater the potential light.

was as taciturn with them as he was with me. But just as often, he would ask someone about the weather or laugh about something that had happened last week. I became caught up in our dynamic, to the point at which I began to go to the deli even on days when I wasn't truly craving a bagel.

My anger toward the deli man grew so great that I would sometimes think about him at night before I fell asleep. Every time I remembered the way he treated me, I was outraged all over again. Fortunately, I was focusing on the Transformation Formula in my Kabbalah studies, and I had recently taken aboard the lesson from the boy copying my tests. So I decided to resist my reactive behavior, but at the same time, I wasn't exactly sure what that implied. Did it mean I should find another deli? There weren't any others nearby. Plus, these were my favorite bagels ever. Did it mean I shouldn't order a bagel on the days this man was working? Or that if he turned out to be my server, I should simply wait for the next one to come along?

None of these solutions felt right. So I decided to continue to go to the deli-on days I was honestly in the mood for a bagel—and to order from whoever was available, but to stop scraping the cream cheese off my bagel in front of this man. Then a strange thing happened: I began to like my bagel with extra cream cheese. Not every day, but on the days this man made my bagel, I found the extra cream cheese soothing. When he was my waitperson, I stopped requesting less cream cheese. I received exactly the same bagel from him that I always had, but I was no longer setting up an obstacle to enjoying the bagel. I was no longer being a victim. Once I no longer took this man's actions personally, I had space to enjoy something new.

After practicing enjoying what the man gave me for several months, I experimented with requesting less cream cheese and gently pointing out to him that he'd put too much on when he loaded it up. He listened, nodded his head, and then said,

life rules

chapter ten: the greater the obstacle, the greater the potential light.

"Thanks for letting me know. I'll remember next time." And he did. But truth be told, I began to miss my heavy dose of cream cheese!

For a moment I wondered if the man had been waiting for me to speak up for myself rather than passive-aggressively trying to punish him, but I let these thoughts go. There is no way to truly know what is going on in the mind of another person. Think how difficult it is to know your own mind! What I didn't let go, however, was the practice of resisting my reactive behavior. In this case it had taken me a while to figure out the hows, but once I had done so, the results were instantaneous and wonderful. I had gained a greater appreciation for life by enjoying my lunch in a new and unexpected way. Plus, I had removed stress from an environment I frequented often. This may sound like a small event in my life, but in fact it was pivotal. It showed me, in everyday terms, the direct connection between Resistance and the Light.

One of the things I began to notice during this time was that the bigger the problem I faced, the stronger was my urge to react. And the bigger my potential reaction, the more Resistance I needed to apply. And the more Resistance I applied, the more Light I allowed into my life. While I can't say that I consciously set out in search of obstacles, my reaction to being faced with them certainly changed. If I could train my mind to respond with kindness and compassion both toward myself and toward the Opponent, then my life would become that much richer.

What I learned with the bagel man I then applied to the teacher who gave me a grade far lower than what I felt I deserved. And to the coach who made me sit out an important basketball game. And to my brother, who borrowed my fountain pen without asking me and then lost it. And to my parents, who, with the best of intentions, had made my life difficult by carving out a path so unlike anyone else's. There were times when I was so

life rules

chapter ten: the greater the obstacle, the greater the potential light.

angry I wanted to punch someone, and times when I was so sad I wanted to curl up into a ball and cry. Then there were times when I was so ecstatically happy, I couldn't sit still. In each case, I fought my reactive behavior. I reminded myself that other people's actions were not personal commentaries on me—and even if they were, that didn't mean I had to react to them, positively or negatively, in any manner that disconnected myself from that particular moment.

Change begins with our willingness to feel what we are going through, and we can't do that if we take ourselves out of the present moment with reactive behavior. To truly transform, we must be open to having a compassionate relationship with all parts of ourselves—even those parts we most dislike, those parts that bring us the most trouble. But how can we get to know these parts when they are always hiding, or yelling, or running away? If we rein in our reactive behavior, then we can sit with it, feel it, get to know it. And by doing so, we can transform it into proactive behavior, which is healing both for ourselves and for others.

My ADD was probably the biggest obstacle I faced in those years, and in many ways that continues to be true today. It's not the kind of thing that just goes away; I had to adapt to it. But once I stopped being so angry with myself and with my lot in life, I was able to appreciate my ADD. Just as I grew to like an onion bagel with extra cream cheese, I learned to appreciate the different paths my ADD took me on. I became a much stronger person for having to learn how to care for myself in particular ways. My ADD also protected me from many potentially dangerous situations. And by having to leave school at painful moments, I stumbled into various adventures and met interesting people. I began to view my ADD as a gift, and I still do.

There is a reason behind everything. And because of this, everything is a gift. The more we understand this, the more we can curb our reactive behavior. And the more we curb our reactive behavior, the more our lives will be filled with the Light in practical terms, learning to resist reactive behavior is like learning any new skill. It takes practice, and you have to start small. It doesn't make sense to wake up tomorrow morning and set about resisting your biggest, most painful reactive behavior. You will need to build up to this. So practice with the girl who cuts you off in the cafeteria line, or the guy who takes your parking space at school. Then gradually move up to folks with whom you have more intimate relationships: best friends, family, perhaps a teacher.

Since I have begun my work as a teacher and author, I have had the honor to know many young men and women in their teens. I have some sense of the issues you are facing, the countless decisions that must be made each day. It's not always clear which situations require Resistance and which don't. So follow your instincts. Pay special attention to those cases when you know something is bad for you, but you decide to do it anyway —or when you get a funny feeling in your stomach that lets you know that something is up. And don't forget that reactive behavior revolves just as much around seemingly positive moments as it does around obstacles. It's all too easy to become addicted to praise or a sense of belonging. By feeling secure or smart or pretty on the basis of a compliment or a sense of inclusion, we are reacting to someone else's sense of us, not our own. And while this is common human behavior, it is also reactive. So as you practice Resistance, be sure to work with compliments as well as insults!

One young woman I know applied the Transformation Formula to a problem she was having with sex. She'd been dating a guy she really liked for a month or so, and he was putting pressure on her. She wanted to have sex too, but not until she got to know him better, and not necessarily in his car to and from school.

He was a charismatic guy, however, and each time they hooked up, she found herself allowing him to go further and further. He

life rules

chapter ten: the greater the obstacle, the greater the potential light.

was her first boyfriend, and she didn't want to disappoint him. Then her grades began to drop, she began fighting more with her parents, and her friends complained that they never saw her. If she had to be really honest with herself, she knew she wasn't ready for sex. But she didn't want to lose her guy. Eventually she realized that every time she had sex with her boyfriend, she was being reactive. She had made him the cause and herself the effect. This ritual they shared of everything from oral sex to a quickie in his car before school gave her a false sense of belonging. She had been reacting to his expectations of her, and by doing so she had closed herself off to the Light. After studying Kabbalah, this girl was able to rethink her relationship with her boyfriend, and she decided that the next time he made a sexual move, she would decline. This was being true to herself. If he broke up with her because of it, so be it. But she knew she needed to become proactive.

It wasn't easy. The following morning, he drove her to school and parked as usual in the dirt road across the way. After a few preliminary kisses, he moved his hand up her skirt—and was stunned and then angry when she removed it. The next day wasn't any better. Or the next. He became increasingly angry with her, but she made sure not to respond reactively. Instead, she told him clearly that while she enjoyed kissing him and light petting, she wasn't enjoying making love and had decided not to do so with him anymore—at least not until things between them matured more naturally. Finally, after a painful breakup that lasted several weeks, he came to her full of remorse and told her that her decision had been the right one, and that he appreciated her strength. He asked if she would consider dating him again if they took things more slowly. She agreed, and many years later they are still happy together.

Not all Resistance stories end in true romance. But often when you give up people and things you once considered precious, the feelings you are looking for come back to you in different ways. For instance, this young woman might have lost this boyfriend for good, even if he had eventually changed his mind—but by being single again, she might have opened herself up to meet a more appropriate guy who was more in tune with her dreams and goals. We have no way of predicting this, but we can experience it. And we experience it by resisting. We are in control of our own lives, but the only way to experience this is through Resistance.

Our society encourages us to seek the path of least resistance, to pursue the easy and comfortable situations in life. We think that by doing so, we are protecting ourselves from suffering and are therefore being kind to ourselves. But in truth, this course only leaves us more fearful and more alienated. It reinforces our sense of being separate, and this separateness acts like a prison. It restricts our ability to care for ourselves and for others, even those closest to us. Curiously, the more we try to shield ourselves from discomfort, the more we suffer. Only by opening ourselves to it can we recognize our kinship to all things. This is what these steps are all about: loving our neighbor—all of our neighbors, not just the ones we like—as ourselves. Staying comfortable doesn't generate lasting Light.

This book is a challenge to leave your comfort zones and to welcome uncomfortable situations. Yes, the path of most Resistance causes pain and discomfort, but after these diminish, we realize that the path of most Resistance is the only way to generate infinite fulfillment, boundless joy, and limitless enlightenment. Suppose God told you that He would give you one million dollars (one million dollars!) every time someone hurt your feelings or angered you—provided that you completely let go of any reactive behavior. Chances are, you would be waking up every morning praying for people to hurt you. And when they did, you would practice the Transformation Formula with all your might. Money is transitory—you spend it, the market eats it up, someone steals it, and so on. But infinite fulfillment goes on forever. And God is offering you this very same bargain. So accept the challenge. The more you resist, the more Light-filled your world will be.

○   Treating yourself and the Opponent with kindness and compassion weakens your ego. It's the "wrong" kind of attention.

○   Resist the urge to take others' words and actions personally, no matter whether they are good, bad, or indifferent.

○   There is a reason behind everything. And because of this, everything is a gift. The better we understand this, the more we will curb our reactive behavior. And the more we curb our reactive behavior, the more our lives will be filled with the Light.

○   Change begins by being in the present moment.

We are seeking the path of most Resistance. Least Resistance leaves us separate from the whole.

Embrace your biggest obstacles; they will reveal the most Light.

Make a list of the last five situations in which you had a strong reaction to an event or a person. Perhaps at this point you are practicing the Transformation Formula. Great! Include those experiences as well, even if they weren't entirely successful. Next, list your reactions (whether you acted on them or resisted them) in order of severity. Did you have your biggest reactions to the most emotionally charged situations and your smallest reactions to less overwhelming situations? Consider the amount of Light you could potentially let into your life by resisting these reactions. In cases where you did resist, explore the relationship between the Light and the size of the obstacle. For instance, did you experience greater Light resisting the situations you marked as being more emotionally charged?

Now make a list of situations in which you habitually react reactively. Someone cuts in front of you getting on the subway. Your friend gets the object you were coveting. A girl you like smiles at you across the hall. Think of specific people you continually tangle with. Your brother, your best friend's other best friend, the guy who rents you videos. List them. Rate them for emotional volatility, from a low of 1 to a high of 10. Circle the lower numbers and begin there. Challenge yourself to resist your reactive behavior daily until you experience changes. Then move up the list until you are tackling your 9's and 10's. Adjust the list as your life changes. Raise your awareness. And be mindful that the higher up the list you move, the greater your access to the Light.

chapter eleven:

when challenges appear overwhelming, inject certainty. the light is always there!

11

11

According to Kabbalah, each of us comes into this world with spiritual baggage from previous lifetimes. This baggage is made up of all the times we failed to resist our reactive behavior, which will need to be corrected at some time in the future. This concept of correction is called "*Tikun.*" It's where we need to do our spiritual work.

We can have a *Tikun* with money, health, or relationships. We know we have stumbled across our personal *Tikun* when a situation feels uncomfortable! If we are intimidated by the popular girls at school, afraid to like something that they don't like, or afraid to dislike something they do, that is our personal *Tikun*—something that needs to be corrected. If we find it difficult to defend our paper to a teacher and thus settle for a grade we feel we didn't deserve, that too is part of a *Tikun*. If we are unable to explain to our parents that we don't want them driving us to the mall anymore because we think we're old enough to walk or take the bus, that's also our *Tikun*.

Look for repetitive behavior. If you are constantly the victim of a situation, or if you are always the abuser, that's a *Tikun*. If we work hard and don't make a penny while our friend slacks off and picks up well-paying jobs, that's a *Tikun* as well. And if we always find ourselves in the same relationship drama, no matter who our partner may be, that too is a *Tikun*.

Unfortunately, when we fail to resist a reactive behavior, it becomes more difficult to correct it the next time around. That particular reactive trait grows stronger. Our Opponent grows stronger. Our *Tikun* will then appear over and over again, through various people in a variety of situations. Initially we may not even recognize the correction in its myriad forms. But the more you work the steps in this book, the easier it will become to identify a particular *Tikun*—even though this time it may take the form of the librarian on a long-winded phone call rather than the waiter with the overly chatty friend. If we are feeling uncom-

life rules

chapter eleven: when challenges appear overwhelming, inject certainty, the light is always there!

fortable in a situation or with a person, then we can be fairly certain we are facing our *Tikun*. And you correct your *Tikun* through Resistance.

With this understanding, we can no longer view ourselves as victims. We simply cannot buy into the notion that life is just happening to us. You and only you have shaped your life thus far. You are shaping it now, right this very second. And your future lies entirely in your hands. Every decision you make influences how your life looks and feels in this new moment, and in all moments yet to come.

Some of you may have seen the film *Groundhog Day*. If you haven't, it's a classic that is well worth renting. It also happens to beautifully illustrate the kabbalistic principle of *Tikun* in action. In this film, Bill Murray plays Phil Connors, a weatherman who is the ultimate reactive character—consumed with himself, conceited and indifferent to the world around him. But Phil gets stuck in a time warp. The day he is living—February 2, or Groundhog Day—keeps repeating itself over and over again, and no one knows this but him.

It's fun at first, as Phil takes advantage of the situation, learning all he can about his world and the people in it in order to manipulate them and serve his own self-interests. But his world turns into a nightmare. Every morning Phil awakens when the momentary pleasures wear off and not a drop of lasting fulfillment is to be found.

Pushed to the point of suicide, he still awakes in the morning to find himself in the same town, confronting the same events. There is no escape—not even death. Finally, Phil decides to change himself, since he cannot change the world around him. He begins to perform good deeds and helps people who are experiencing the same misfortunes each day.

Suddenly, he feels true fulfillment. Inspired by this Light, he goes on a rampage of sharing all over town, winning the hearts of everyone. Eventually the nightmare ends and he finds himself in a brand-new day, arm in arm with the woman of his dreams. This is *Tikun*. This is the reason our lives sometimes feel as if we are trapped in a bad movie.

We are on Step Eleven so chances are you've been practicing these steps as you go along. That's wonderful! I'd like to take some time now for fine tuning. With this step we are honing in on the subtleties of Resistance via our individual *Tikun*. Therefore, let's take a closer look at the subject of Resistance as it relates to our individual *Tikun*.

Resisting Laziness

You are happily lying on your couch doing absolutely nothing when the scene you need for the short story you're working on pops into your head. You're excited, but you're so comfortable that you can't seem to get off the couch. You convince yourself that you will remember the idea (even though you know you won't) and settle back into those big, soft cushions. Resist this laziness! Resistance doesn't necessarily imply stopping and standing still. Often it means stopping the desire to stop and diving in head first. Here, your *Tikun* consists of not being able to finish what you start.

Resisting Ego

Let's say you and a group of schoolmates have just finished a photography class. Everyone is talking, showing off their expertise. Your mother happens to be a professional photographer, and you practically grew up in the darkroom, so it's obvious to you that you know much more than they do about the subject. You feel an urge to speak and flaunt your knowledge. Resist! This is your ego at work. Your *Tikun* may be a feeling of superiority. Don't say a word. Recognize the spiritual opportunity and let it go. The Light will enter, and you may learn something valuable from the conversation.

Resisting Judgment

You walk into the school bathroom to discover your two best friends having a major fight. One friend storms out. The other fills you in on his side of the story. You're appalled! You are ready to pass judgment and choose sides. Resist! Let go of your emotions. Wait for your other friend to tell you his side. Your *Tikun* is probably connected to judgmental behavior. You will discover that there are two sides to every story.

Resisting Self-Involvement

You've been accepted at three of the four colleges you applied to, and you can't make up your mind which one to attend. You run through lists of the pros and cons. You ask your mother for insight. Then your father. Then your sister, even though she's still in grade school. You spend evenings on the phone getting opinions from your friends. Everyone has different advice. Soon you are a bundle of stress and are no closer to a satisfactory decision. Resist the urge to wallow in your anguish. Go out and do something good for someone else. Spend a little time helping others with their problems. When you get out of your own way, answers will come to you when you least expect them.

Resisting Evil Impulses

You woke up with a pimple on the tip of your nose, messed up on your math test, and then had a fight with your boyfriend. All in one day! You're feeling blue and insecure. Then a friend calls and, after a bit of small talk, begins bad-mouthing a girl you both know. You join in. Pointing out someone else's faults makes you feel like less of a loser! Hearing about someone else's troubles make you feel better about your own lousy day. Resist the desire to gossip and speak badly of others! Kabbalistically, the sin of murder is not limited to physical death; it also includes character assassination. When we speak unkindly of our friends, we are symbolically killing them. Ending the conversation, or changing the subject, is therefore the equivalent of saving someone's life. This will reveal tremendous Light, which is what will truly help with your problems.

Resisting Control

You've been receiving lots of praise for your paintings in art class, so your mother shows them to her friend, who runs a prestigious art gallery in the city. You think your paintings are pretty good, so you respond with enthusiasm. But your mother's friend thinks your painting needs lots of work before it's ready for the marketplace. You take this hard-hitting critique personally and begin to lose your confidence. Resist! Your reaction means you believe that you're the true source of this art, not the Light. Great artists know that they are just channels. Moreover, even the criticism comes from the Light. So give up control. Trust the process and let go of your personal attachment to your work.

Resisting Expectations

You have helped your friend with his homework every single day for two weeks, so you expect that when you need him to help you clean out your parents' garage, he will do so. Instead, he has another commitment. You are finally getting to go away on spring break with your classmates. You expect it to be sunny every day, but instead it rains. You have begun smoking pot after school with the cool kids. You expect them to be nicer to you now. They're not. You have lost 15 pounds by throwing up the majority of your meals. You expect that boys will now ask you out. And they do, but not the ones you really like. Resist all your feelings of disappointment! Stop those feelings of victimization. Something better is coming. Embrace the kabbalistic principle of asking the Light for what you need in life, not for what you want. Later, you will see the hidden blessing and the spiritual reason for what now seems so disappointing.

Resisting a Lack of Confidence

You've been selected by your teacher to give a speech at the end-of-year presentation, which requires speaking into a microphone in front of several hundred people. Your natural reaction is, "I can't do it; I'm not good enough. I don't want all that attention focused on me." This is reverse ego at work, but it's still ego. Let go of your limited thinking. It's not all about you. There's a bigger picture here that includes other people. Focus on finding a way to help them get what they need, and you'll find yourself succeeding effortlessly.

Resisting Insecurity

You and a friend worked long and hard on an after-school project. The class loved it. The teacher was so impressed that she asked the principal if it could be put on special display in the main hall. Now you're reluctant to share too much credit. You try to calculate who did what, giving yourself the benefit of every doubt. What if everyone thinks your friend was the major contributor to the project? Resist those reactive thoughts and feelings! Then give away all the credit. All of it. Let go completely. A little voice inside may start telling you, *I can resist, but not too much; I need to practice this Kabbalah stuff one step at a time.* Nonsense! Resist these thoughts as well, and give all the credit to your partner. Remember, the Opponent will test you every step of the way. Praise gives pleasure for a moment, but the Light remains eternal. Don't trade away the farm for a bit of ego gratification.

Resisting Embarrassment

In the middle of choir practice, the teacher waves her hands for the singing to stop. Everyone sees her but you. You keep singing a few bars at the top of your lungs, all by yourself, and singing on key is not your strong point. You turn six shades of purple and want to fall into a hole. You try desperately to cover up your embarrassment. Resist! Love the humiliation. Take it all in. Lower your defenses. Lower your guard. Walk through the mishap slowly, and soak up as much embarrassment as possible. Make yourself vulnerable. At the end of the day, your ego will have been put in its place, which is a good thing, and no one will even remember your error. Or perhaps you will even be able to turn it into a moment that everyone thought was funny and enjoyed. That's how the Light works.

Resisting the Need to Be Admired

You're at a party with school friends, and you're meeting kids from another school. You're introduced as the "smart one" in your group, so now you feel pressure to respond to difficult questions even when you're not sure of the answers. You start to fake it. Resist! Just say, "I don't know." Leave it at that. Then resist those reactive thoughts that tell you that your friends might not like, admire, or look up to you anymore.

Resisting Doubts

You apply the wisdom of Kabbalah in your life. You use the principle of Resistance in a real-life situation, but with no results. Doubts flood your mind. It doesn't work, you say to yourself. Resist these reactive thoughts! This is just a test to see if you've truly surrendered. Whenever you look for results, you're missing the point of the exercise. That's the paradox: Look for results and they won't come. Give it up and you'll get it all!

What each of these scenarios has in common is the possibility of feeling overwhelmed. The way to counter this is to inject certainty. But what does that mean? Most of you are probably familiar with the story of Moses leading the Israelites out of bondage. Pharaoh and his army had chased the Israelites right to the edge of the Red Sea, where it seemed they had met their end. But Moses led his people into the sea, and he led them so far that their garments were soaked and their noses and ears were filled with water. No one was without fear—not even Moses. Moses called out to God for help, to which God responded, "Why are you calling out to me?" In response, Moses and his people set aside their fears and continued on. And sure enough, before the water could drown them, it parted and rose high above their heads, allowing them to easily flee the approaching Egyptians. As Pharaoh's army raced into the seabed in hot pursuit of the Israelites, the sea fell, and countless soldiers were drowned.

life rules

chapter eleven: when challenges appear overwhelming, inject certainty, the light is always there!

According to Kabbalah, this entire story is a code. "Egypt" is a code word for our material existence in this physical world of chaos, or the 1% Realm. "Pharaoh" is code for the human ego and humanity's incessantly reactive, self-seeking, intolerant nature. Any aspect of our nature that controls us is Pharaoh! As for God's mysterious answer to Moses' plea—*Why are you calling out to me?*—Kabbalah teaches that concealed within this question is a profound spiritual truth: God did not part the Red Sea. In fact, God was surprised that Moses even called upon Him at that moment. Moses and his people parted that sea. And they did it by injecting certainty.

Another thing these scenarios share is Temptation. The Opponent flashes instant gratification in front of us each time we let him. All too often we accept, because reactive behavior is extremely tempting. As we've discussed with the short-circuiting light bulb, the burst of light supplied by instant gratification is intense. Most of the time it's much brighter than the consistent Light supplied by Resistance. If we forget this for even one moment, we can easily be seduced into doing anything. Drugs, alcohol, and sex are all like short-circuiting light bulbs. And each will leave you in the dark the second the light has burned out.

A young man, James, began visiting our Centre several years ago. He was in his teens and was very handsome and popular at school. He played several sports and was the captain of the football team. He had a nice girlfriend, and his parents seemed involved in his life. Regardless of all this, James viewed himself as a misfit. He thought his body had become too big from all the athletics, and that his girlfriend liked him only because his parents were rich. Everyone was expecting James to go on to a good college, most likely on a football scholarship, after which he would probably take over his dad's thriving car dealership. But James had little desire to do any of these things. What he really wanted to be was an artist. He wasn't even sure what kind of artist, because he'd never been given the opportunity to explore it—but he liked the idea of moving to a big city after high school, living in a studio with lots of natural sunlight, hanging out at cafés and bars, and creating great art that would make people respect his mind, not just his body. James had shared his dreams with his girlfriend, his parents, and some of his good friends, but no one took him seriously. So he continued along in a life that met other people's expectations. But as a result, his own unhappiness, frustration, and loneliness grew larger and larger. He felt trapped and misunderstood, incapable of acting on his true needs.

One night at a party, a kid James didn't know well offered him some coke. James had smoked pot a couple of times before and hadn't really liked it. He also knew that an athlete should steer clear of drugs, but he was tired of doing the right thing. And he was also tired of feeling lousy. So he snorted one line and then another. Sure enough, in no time he felt great. He walked around the party chatting easily with everyone—even the painters and photographers whom he'd always been hesitant to approach. In the weeks that followed, James did more coke. He began buying his own supply rather than relying on others. He began to lose weight, which made him happy but infuriated his coach. His academic performance fell off a bit, but nothing disastrous. And his girlfriend complained that he was acting funny, but she didn't leave him.

James liked everything about the drug—the ease with which he could converse with all sorts of people, the fearlessness he felt, and the overall boost he received to his self-esteem. But the mornings after a night of partying were the worst. Everything felt wrong. He was overwhelmed with grief and guilt and despair. Often he tried to lie in bed and avoid the world altogether, but his parents forced him to go to school. Eventually he found that if he did a line or two in the bathroom in the morning, it would help settle his feelings of worthlessness and outrage. Not long after this, the football coach booted him off the team, his

life rules

chapter eleven: when challenges appear overwhelming, inject certainty, the light is always there!

girlfriend dumped him, and his parents grounded him for two weeks.

James had created a situation for himself that we all create in one way or another. He'd become dependent on an external force—in this case, drugs—to bring inner peace. The problem here is that this doesn't work. It's simply not possible. Furthermore, although James believed that he was protecting himself from pain and suffering, he was actually adding to his misery by heightening his sense of separateness. He had dug himself a terrible hole. Sure, the drugs supplied instant gratification. They short-circuited his energy, and in that moment the intensity of the Light was like nothing he'd ever experienced before. But darkness came the morning after, and it was too painful to bear. So James became even more addicted to quick hits of the Light, hoping that if he found a way to string enough of them together, he would be okay. This is a false hope we all set up for ourselves.

I'm happy to be able to report to you that James finally cleaned himself up. The only way he could overcome what had become a nasty drug habit was to apply Resistance. He had to constantly remind himself that while there was pleasure to be had, that pleasure came and went, and the ensuing loss of Light was debilitating. He used the ideas in this book to help himself. Whenever he felt overwhelmed—which was often—he injected certainty. He did away with all expectations, for himself and his friends and his family. He forced himself to stay in the moment and experience it fully—all the aches and pains, all the incredible sadness and guilt and fear, and all the exhilaration and excitement. He let these complex feelings coexist, understanding that one does not overrule another. Life is paradox.

James has been clean now for several years. Interestingly, when he first stopped using, he stumbled in an unexpected way. Things became very good for him almost right away. His parents treated him to a long vacation in Europe, and when he returned, he met a wonderful girl and fell in love. During his recovery, James had begun to dabble in ceramics and was accepted to a good art school, not on the basis of his athletic prowess but on the merits of his artistic talent. In addition to this, he began volunteering at a local community center to help kids who were trying to get off drugs. All in all, he felt extraordinarily lucky and fulfilled.

But James fell into a new trap. It didn't involve drugs, and in that sense nothing "bad" happened to him. But James became as addicted to praise as he had been to drugs. In both cases, he was unduly swayed by external influences. He needed to begin working on the resistance of expectations again, this time from a different angle.

If you want to see real miracles in your own life, try shutting down thoughts of uncertainty. Put your focus on removing Bread of Shame instead. Think of James. Once he seized the opportunity to remove Bread of Shame and transform from reactive to proactive, James accomplished the original objective of the Vessel—to become the cause of his own fulfillment. Once this feat had been achieved, the Light was allowed to flow freely. James remained off drugs and was able to tap into his true desire: art. By staying in an uncomfortable situation, he was able to face one of his *Tikuns* and transform it. But notice that after the transformation took place, there were still more awaiting him. Be careful not to become addicted to the notion that one Resistance will fix everything. This process is ongoing. You have your whole life to perfect it. But as your ability to resist grows stronger, you will notice changes all around you.

Keep in mind that injecting certainty does not mean that you get what you want. It is not a matter of walking around repeating, "I want a brand-new blue electric guitar" and being certain that you will get it. Injecting certainty means that you will get what you need. It's like the Rolling Stones lyric, "You can't always get what you want, but if you try sometimes, you just might find you get what you need." Sometimes what you want is what you need and sometimes it's not. But certainty allows you to accept responsibility for whatever negativity and positivity appear in your life. You planted that seed at some point in your past—of this there is no doubt.

When you overcome your uncertainty, you create miracles in your life.

○   We carry the seeds of our past thoughts, words, and actions with us. This is our *Tikun*. We generate it whenever we avoid Resistance. Repetitive and uncomfortable patterns are a good indication we've stumbled into one.

○   Resistance takes many forms; sometimes it may be physically active while at other times it may be purely internal. Heightened awareness is key to recognizing situations clearly.

○   Injecting certainty into overwhelming situations allows for miracles to occur in your life.

○   Certainty does not mean you get what you want; it means you get what you need.

Consider the various Resistance stories you've read. Write down any experiences you've had that may be similar to these. As always, use as much detail as you can. What was your mental and physical response to these situations? Were you having any intuitive hunches that you overlooked? List at least two ways in which you could have injected certainty into each situation. Consider what the outcome might have been. Would you have gotten the results you wanted? How about the results you needed? What might the difference have been?

11

true internal change is created through the DNA power of the Hebrew letters.

12

12

When I was in high school, one of the kids in my class kept dying his hair. One week it was jet black, the next a sort of yellowish-orange that I suppose was meant to be blonde. He even snuck in a few hot pinks and blues, but the teachers didn't tolerate those very well. The kid's natural color was a deep chestnut brown, not unattractive at all—but by dying his hair, he was experimenting. All in all, it was not a bad way to figure some things out—much safer than drugs and guns, for instance. Yet no matter what color he chose, within a couple of weeks his brown roots would reappear.

I remember discussing this kid's hair with my parents—I'd been making a pitch to dye mine as well—and my father felt that the situation contained a useful analogy. The hair dye, according to my father, represented external change and was therefore not unlike all the machinations we go through to avoid suffering and find happiness. But it couldn't last. The kid I knew had brown hair as a result of his DNA, which was internal. My father asked me to consider how many times I had attempted to initiate change in my behavior only to find myself reverting back to my old ways. I was disconcerted to admit that this was the case most of the time. Did anyone, I wondered, have the emotional and spiritual strength to permanently stop their internal reactions dead in their tracks? Or possess the foresight to see beyond the immediate moment and not become upset or panicky when a nasty problem arose? My father's answer was no. No individual has such power. I was very put out by this. By that point I had spent a lot of time and energy taking responsibility for my thoughts, words, and actions and had been practicing Resistance as much as I could. I was feeling liberated, even exhilarated, by the thought that my fate lay entirely within my hands, so I was quite deflated to hear that I was incapable of making these changes stick. Just like this kid's roots, my DNA would surface again.

life rules

chapter twelve: true internal change is created through the DNA power of the Hebrew letters.

Quickly, my father let me know that Kabbalah provided help that would strike at the deepest root level of our existence. Its impact was lasting. Earlier we defined the 99% Realm as the DNA level of our reality, as the cause of all causes. Then we discussed the fact that when the Satan came into being, he reconfigured the DNA of the Desire to Receive into the Desire to Receive for the Self Alone. So we now have a loose working notion of DNA. But what is it, really?

DNA is best described as an instruction manual for our cells. All cells begin in an undifferentiated state. Our DNA then determines which cells will evolve to become internal organs, bones, brain matter, or other tissues. Like all instruction manuals, DNA is written in a language that is composed of an alphabet. In this case it's a code—one that was cracked in the late 1950s by geneticists who determined that the DNA alphabet is composed of four "letters," which they designated A, T, C, and G. These letters combine to form "words" and "sentences" that comprise the genetic code of every individual. We each have about three billion letters in our genetic codes. The differences between us lie in the combination and sequences of these four letters. And each cell in our body contains the whole three-billion-letter instruction booklet. So in a physical sense, all we are is a walking, talking, breathing set of letters!

In truth, the entire universe is alphabetical in nature. Just as letters combine to form words, atoms combine to create more complicated structures known as molecules. Just as words combine to form sentences, molecules combine to create various kinds of matter. All of this information about DNA and the alphabetically structured universe was discovered only within the last 50 years. Remarkably, however, Abraham wrote about these very things some 4,000 years ago in *The Book of Formation*. Here Abraham posited that the entire universe consisted of building blocks. Moreover, he said that these building blocks were alphabetical in nature! Abraham went on to reveal how the

Light of the Creator had fragmented into 22 distinct forces in order to create our universe. These 22 forces are actually 22 letters.

These ancient characters are no ordinary letters; they are brimming with transformative power. In fact, these letters of the Hebrew alphabet were present at the very moment of creation. Be careful not to limit your understanding of these letters. They are magnificent engines of primordial energy. They appear as both shapes and vibrations that we can visualize as well as vocalize. In fact, the Hebrew word for *letter* actually means "pulse" or "vibration."

By virtue of their shapes, sounds, and vibrations, these letters arouse and harness the energy of the universe. Some of the world's greatest thinkers—scientists, philosophers, mathematicians, and physicians, not to mention many great painters, writers, and musicians—have tapped into the power of the Hebrew alphabet.

A doctor friend of mine, Dr. Artur Spokojny, had a profound experience with these letters. A board-certified internist and cardiologist, Dr. Spokojny studied medicine at Harvard and graduated summa cum laude from Düsseldorf University in Germany. Spokojny, who was instrumental in developing laser treatments for heart disease, holds a faculty position at Cornell Medical College and maintains privileges at New York Presbyterian Hospital. Since 1988, he has been assistant director of the Catheterization Center at New York Hospital. I'm providing you with these impressive credentials only to dissuade you from writing off the amazing experience I'm about to describe!

One evening a patient was rushed into the emergency room with a heart attack. Although the patient was conscious, his heart was slow, and Dr. Spokojny was understandably worried—so he asked that the patient be taken to the lab. The patient's heart actually stopped twice en route. As it turned out, his right coronary artery was completely blocked. Dr. Spokojny and his team worked on the man for nearly an hour, but nothing did the trick. Whatever they tried—and they tried everything—failed. Dr. Spokojny later told me that he felt absolutely helpless, and this filled him with despair. So he decided to meditate on a sequence of Hebrew letters that are used for healing.

The moment Dr. Spokojny began visualizing the letters, he could feel something happening. Suddenly, the blocked artery opened! He and his team were shocked. Their patient had a massive blood clot in his artery, which in all truth should have prevented the artery from opening. More spectacular still, when the whole ordeal was over, there was absolutely no damage to the man's heart. None. Not a hint of evidence of a heart attack. When Dr. Spokojny later spoke with the patient, the man told him that he had dreamed he was trapped inside a computer monitor. All the exit doors were locked shut. Suddenly, he found the right sequence of letters for the password. It opened the doors, and he escaped. Later still, my friend discussed the episode with the other doctors involved. No one had any explanation for what had occurred. Technically their patient should have been dead. Dr. Spokojny was unwilling to tell them what he had done, and the medical mystery remained unsolved.

As you can see, these ancient Hebrew letters contain enormous amounts of spiritual influence. They can supply us with the emotional power and inner strength we need to overcome our reactive behavior. Moreover, different combinations of letters create different blends of energy, just as different combinations of musical notes create different melodies. The Light they emit purifies our hearts. Their spiritual influences cleanse destructive impulses from our being. Their sacred energy removes rash, intolerant emotions as well as fear and anxiety. They can promote healing, financial sustenance, and emotional well-being.

Most likely you haven't the faintest idea how to read Hebrew. No worries. The power can be transmitted to us merely by scanning the letters in much the same way that a scanner reads a bar code. We can deepen the experience by meditating on the letters, as Dr. Spokojny did. Ancient sages considered the eyes to be the window to the soul. Therefore, looking at these letters in any way provides us with a direct connection to our souls as well as to the 99% Realm. When we scan, meditate, and visually interact with these letters, not only do we access the remaining major segment of our consciousness, but our subconscious absorbs the power and spiritual influences emanating from each word.

The human soul and the forces contained within the Hebrew letters are both formed from the blazing Light of the Creator. When the two are in proximity—achieved by visually scanning, meditating, or reciting the letters—a resonance is created, and the energy of the letters is duplicated in the soul. These letters can help us in all aspects of our lives; nothing is beyond their reach. And by working with them, our transformations become lasting rather than temporary. In order to return to the 99% Realm, to return home, we must diligently transform our reactive nature in every area of our lives. And in order to accomplish that, we've been given a set of tools that are as old as time itself. It starts with the 72 Names of God.

There are three prerequisites to activating the power of the 72 Names:

1. Conviction in their power;
2. An understanding of the particular influence radiating from each Name; and
3. A follow-through physical action to activate their power.

The first prerequisite is up to you. Your ego will do its darnedest to make you doubt the power of these letters. Yet the more reactive we remain, the more powerful our ego becomes. Engaging and winning this battle is the ultimate purpose of life. Remember, this is how you find the Light.

The second prerequisite is provided for you. The spiritual influence and power of each Name are now yours to access after countless decades of secrecy. Appreciating this fact will further enrich your connection to the Light.

The third requirement is sometimes the hardest one to meet. To give an example, if you are using a particular Name to triumph over your fear of heights, you will have to confront that fear in order to eradicate it from your life. You will have to climb to the top of the tallest building you know of and look down. It's a simple physical action that flips on the "Light switch." But you should know that when you confront your fear with your new-found spiritual strength, you will conquer it, and you'll be well on your way to a life free from fear.

In addition to questioning why Moses was calling upon Him for help, God instructed Moses and his people to "go jump in the water." Here the Israelites were being required to activate the power of the 72 Names by performing step three: the physical act of confronting their fears. Before and during the act of wading into the waters, Moses and the Israelites meditated on a sequence from the 72 Names that they believed would help them. By meditating, they were expressing their conviction, or injecting their certainty—and by walking into the treacherous waters, they were activating the breathtaking spiritual force of these 72 Names by performing a physical action. This is important stuff. Moses and his people can serve as role models for all of us. What is clear from this coded reading of Exodus is that God never answers prayers; instead, He helps us figure out how to answer our own prayers! We do so by learning how to connect to and utilize the divine energy of the Creator and the Godlike force in our own souls.

The power of the Hebrew letters is primordial; it surpasses any intellectual understanding. Once you have had a chance to familiarize yourself with the letters, you may want to deepen the experience and meditate on them.

To do so, find a quiet setting—one where you are least likely to be disturbed by curious siblings or concerned parents, faithful pets or bored friends. Then take a few moments to make sure the area is clean and neat. You want to be respectful of both yourself and the lineage of these letters. Now, take a seat in a comfortable chair or, if you prefer, sit on the floor. Next, consider what has inspired you to turn to this power at this particular moment. What Red Sea are you facing? What army of Pharaoh's is approaching from behind?

Once you are feeling settled, decide on which letter sequence most closely pertains to your concern or aspiration at this moment. Scan the letters, and then read the accompanying text. Now allow your eyes to gently rest on the letters with full attention, but without undue focus or concentration. Try not to let your attention wander or sink. Whenever it does, gently bring it back to the letters. Sometimes it's helpful to focus on the breath—on inhaling and exhaling and inhaling again. You can even imagine that you are inhaling the power of the letters and that this power is filling every molecule of your body. Then, when you exhale, imagine you are exhaling the power out for others to access. Then, breathe in the power once more—perhaps in the form of golden light—and let it fill you. Keep doing this until your breathing and visualizations feel natural and easy. Then close your eyes and see the letters in your mind's eye. Try to imagine them as vividly as possible, just as if you were looking at them on the page. See the black letters outlined against a white background. Then open your eyes.

Once more, focus on the letters. Use your breathing practice to inhale and exhale the Light. Continue this for a comfortable

life rules

chapter twelve: true internal change is created through the DNA power of the Hebrew letters.

interval. Close your eyes once again and visualize the letters, but this time imagine them as white against a black background. Let them fill your mind as completely as possible. If other thoughts or images arise, don't get upset; just return to your breath until they drift away. Be aware now that the letters are no longer on the paper; they are within you! Whenever you feel the desire, open your eyes. Resist the urge to study the letters some more. For the time being, the printed letters are irrelevant. The letters are within you now. Actually, they've always been within you; they've simply been reawakened.

Remember to approach your obstacles as opportunities to reveal the Light. If you attempt this practice expecting that your current situation will become more comfortable, you will be sadly disappointed; more than likely, the present circumstances will reappear until you understand things differently. There is nothing wrong with changing the color of your hair, by the way. Life is fun; we should enjoy it. But for any lasting change, we need to go to the root. This book shows you how to access that power—power you've always carried within you but perhaps never knew was there. In order to enjoy it, you must earnestly, diligently, and compassionately work these steps. This chapter supplies you with the most precious of magic tools: knowledge of the Hebrew letters. Treat them with the respect they deserve.

Complete 72 Names Chart

כהת	אכא	ללה	מהש	עלם	סיט	ילי	והו
הקם	הרי	מבה	יזל	ההע	לאו	אלד	הזי
וזו	מלה	ייי	נלך	פהל	לוו	כלי	לאו
ושר	לכב	אום	ריי	שאה	ירת	האא	נתה
ייז	רהע	חעם	אני	מנד	כוק	להו	יוו
מיה	עשל	ערי	סאל	ילה	וול	מיכ	ההה
פוי	מבה	נית	נגא	עמם	הוש	דני	והו
מוי	עלו	יהה	ומב	מצר	הרח	ייל	נמם
מום	היי	יבמ	ראה	חבו	איע	מנק	דמב

196

○ No matter how profound they may be, our external changes will never last. We must alter our DNA in order to achieve lasting change.

○ No individual has the power to change their DNA permanently. Only scanning the 72 Names of God can accomplish this.

○ The letters release enormous amounts of spiritual influence; they supply us with emotional power and inner strength.

○ Scanning letters provides a direct but subconscious connection to our souls and to the 99% Realm.

Science has recognized that human beings make use of only 10% of our full potential consciousness. When we scan, meditate, and visually interact with the letters, we access the remaining major segment of our consciousness.

By meditating on these potent letters, you are able to access the Light that is within you, the Light that has always been within you, the Light that comes from the Creator.

We repeat circumstances until we figure out how to transform them.

Make a list of three things about yourself you would most like to transform. Consider why you'd like to transform these things. Are you merely trying to escape from suffering? Or do you view these aspects of yourself as opportunities to reveal the Light? Now review the three prerequisites to engaging the power of the 72 Names of God. Consider how strong or tentative your conviction might be in their power. How can you enhance your position? For each fear that you are facing, jot down one or two follow-through actions that will help to activate the letters. Be thoughtful in your choices. Don't go for the easy out, rather consider options that will encourage you to truly eradicate these fears. This will help prepare you for the moment you meet with the letters.

all of the negative
traits that you spot in
others are merely a
reflection of your own
negative traits. only
by fixing yourself can
you change others.

13

13

once knew a guy in junior high school who always wanted something from me. I appreciated the fact that he took the time to speak with me, and he often asked probing questions about my life that made me feel as if he actually cared. Invariably, however, he'd need to borrow a pencil or was hoping to catch a ride home with my mother—or, on one occasion, he wanted to borrow the one really nice sweater I had to wear to a football game so that he could talk to a girl he liked. This guy never thanked me for anything he borrowed or for any of the efforts I made to help him out. And whatever he borrowed never seemed to be enough. The same held true of my good deeds. He was insatiable, and I was exhausting and frustrating myself trying to provide for him.

As the days and weeks rolled by, I became more and more annoyed by this guy. I found myself keeping a mental list of all the ways in which he was taking advantage of me. Honestly, he was a nice enough guy, but he was so needy! And so ungrateful. During this same time frame, if there wasn't basketball practice after school, I used to spend the rest of my day hanging around The Kabbalah Centre talking to people who came there. I enjoyed spending my time with these folks, who were all extremely kind and often remarkably knowledgeable. As you know, I often felt out of place at school, but none of those feelings arose with this group. I felt comfortable talking to them about whatever was troubling me.

I remember one man, to whom I often spoke about my greater fears and hopes, saying with great affection, "Yehuda, you want so much. You are like a great big well that cannot ever be properly filled because you have sprung a leak somewhere deep." Naturally, I was not thrilled by this observation, so I began to avoid this man, to whom I had often been turning for guidance.

Meanwhile, at school, my friend wanted to copy my notes from science lab, and trade parts of his lunch for mine, and have me go to a party with him because the captain of the hockey team would be there. And for some reason, the more he kept after me at school, the harder it was for me to face the man at The Centre!

Eventually, in my studies with my father, my brother and I got to the ideas in this chapter. And when we did, a light bulb went on in my head! I recognized the same behavior in my classmate that I had been exhibiting at the Centre. Even though I hadn't felt that I was being needy in my interactions there, I had developed an expectation that these people would always be there for me, that they would always listen and always help. No wonder I hadn't been able to face that man! I had thought I was angry with him, but I was merely attempting to dodge an aspect of myself that I wasn't keen to look at.

Owning up to our negative traits is never easy. It is much, much easier to spot the faults of others and complain about them. Recognizing those traits in ourselves can be embarrassing, frustrating, and even painful. This is why we must be extremely gentle with ourselves during this process. Remind yourself that none of these steps is about judgment. Judgment is a reactive behavior even when you are applying it to yourself. Gently observe yourself. If you are having a hard time seeing yourself clearly at this point, then consider the traits in others with which you struggle the most. Chances are you have some variations of these traits in yourself. Discovering these traits is nothing to be ashamed of. Instead, it's a reason for celebration. Without obstacles—which is what our negative traits are—we would have nothing to transform and would therefore be cut off from the Light. Owning up to obstacles—taking responsibility for them and applying these steps to them—is challenging. But if we do not do so, we are keeping ourselves trapped in our unhappy prisons. What a relief to find out that we hold the key, and now we know how to use it!

When I discussed my insight with my father, he reminded me that I shouldn't get too attached to locating my negative traits and transforming them. We have to be mindful not to let our egos butt in and encourage us to indulge in spiritual witch-hunting with our own souls as the target. Negative traits are human. They are opportunities to transform, not opportunities to beat ourselves up.

My father compared negative character traits to a mirror that reflected all of our reactive instincts back at us. Imagine that the mirror shattered, my father said, into 1,000 little pieces that floated out into the universe. All the negative people, all the negative situations and obstacles that you confront, all the things you see wrong in others, are merely pieces of that mirror. When you manage to transform a particular piece of your character, one of the fragments of the mirror will reflect this change! You will then begin to see the positive aspects of other people. And situations in your life will begin to change for the better.

There is nothing we can do to actually change another human being. We can provide help on physical, mental, emotional, or spiritual levels; we can attempt to influence people in ways we think would benefit them; and we can try to act in a manner and make decisions that would serve as positive models. But ultimately we cannot transform anyone else's obstacles—not even if we love them more than any other person on this planet. This is important to understand. We spend a lot of our time trying to change others, for reasons that vary from kindness right through to control. But regardless of our motivation, attempting to change another person is a losing battle. (Think how hard it is to change yourself, the person you know best of all!) And even if you could change another person, you would only leave them with Bread of Shame. They need to bring change on their own.

Many, many people wear themselves out trying to change others, and in the process forget all about themselves. I knew a young woman at The Kabbalah Centre named Virginia. While in high school, Virginia had begun dating this guy, Ed, whom she was crazy about. I met him a couple of times, and he was very nice. He was smart and funny and was extremely kind to her. They clearly shared great affection. But Ed drank too much. If they went to parties together, Virginia would be afraid to ride home with him behind the wheel. Sometimes he would act inappropriately in public, fondling her to the point at which it made her uncomfortable. On other nights, he would refuse to leave events at their agreed-upon time because he just wanted to have another drink.

Ed's behavior while sober was quite different from his behavior while inebriated. He never hurt Virginia or threatened to hurt her, and he wasn't drunk on a regular basis. So Virginia convinced herself that she could get Ed to change—that under her care, his life would get back on track again. She tried everything. One night she cried for hours, telling Ed that if he really loved her, he would stop drinking. On another occasion, she calmly explained how it felt to be in a relationship with Ed; she even came up with some parallel illustrations from his life that she thought would help him understand her feelings more clearly. One night she flipped out on him, screaming and yelling and calling him names. Another time she simply got wasted with him. None of this changed Ed's drinking. None of it seemed to even influence him. All of her efforts served only to exhaust Virginia. She was taking Ed's drinking personally, and because of that, her behavior was entirely reactive. He was her cause; she was his effect.

Once she realized this, Virginia began to put the focus on herself. What steps could she take that could make her situation more fulfilling? First she made a distinction between herself and Ed. She grew to understand that Ed's drinking had nothing whatsoever to do with her. This was very liberating. Once Virginia recognized this, she was able to approach Ed with compassion and kindness rather than with anger and frustration whenever she found that he was drinking. Without this attachment to her expectations, Virginia was able to realize that nothing she could do would free Ed from his personal pain and obstacles. He was in charge of his life, just as she was in charge of hers. Eventually Virginia broke up with Ed, but she always kept a special place for him in her heart.

While it's true that you cannot make changes for another person, you can by all means serve as a living example, a role model, and a beacon of Light. This can serve to draw others to the wisdom of Kabbalah. Teaching Kabbalah, however, does not mean preaching Kabbalah. To teach means to share this wisdom with others out of a genuine desire to share something that you found helpful, not because you want to convert someone. Or convince someone. Or sell to someone. World peace begins at home, with personal peace. But as we begin to experience the Light, we find ourselves naturally wanting to share it with others.

Not a day passes when I am not aware of the great kindness of my mother and father. During times when they were desperately in need of help from others, they were in fact helping others. Please don't get the impression that my parents are superheroes. They feel pain as deeply as you or I do. But during these particularly lean years, it did take great commitment—and great certainty—for them to raise a family, establish The Kabbalah Centre, and remain attentive to one another. It's not that my mother and father were born with extraordinary patience, endurance, and compassion. They just worked hard to improve their lives and the lives of those around them. They identified and faced their obstacles; they injected certainty; they scanned and meditated on the Hebrew letters; and they refused to let their egos win the battle for control of their souls.

According to the ancient kabbalists, the Hebrew year of 5760 (the year 2000 in the Western calendar) would usher in a new era that *The Zohar* describes with two words: Woe and Blessed.

Woe refers to a time of great upheaval, terror, and pain, affecting us both personally and globally. During this time, the immune system of humankind will be under attack. Diseases both new and old will torment us. There will be global wars and acts of terror, as well as the destruction of our environment. But it is through these global and personal tragedies that humanity will come to realize that treasures procured through the ego are illusionary and fleeting. And come at a high cost.

The Zohar also calls this era Blessed. This refers to a time of peace, tranquillity, enlightenment, and eternal fulfillment. Disease will be decimated. Chaos will no longer exist. Joy will be everywhere.

We have been given a choice.

Violence in the world is not aimless chaos. Disease is not a haphazard occurrence. Terrorism is not random madness. Earthquakes are not acts of God. All these negative phenomena are born within the darkness that is created when our collective reactive behavior disconnects us all from the 99% Realm. Grasping this difficult truth is the prerequisite to effecting true change.

The state of the world is merely the sum total of the interactions of humanity. Black holes in space, tornados in Oklahoma, drive-by shootings, tater tots for school lunch, sunny days, unwanted pregnancies, peace among nations, available parking spots—everything depends on the interactions between one human being and another. When the ancient sages declared that the earth is the center of the universe, they were not speaking about physical coordinates. They were speaking in spiritual terms. Our spiritual actions, be they reactive or proactive, drive the cosmos.

The simple reactive act of yelling at your friend, speaking abusively to your little sister, or cheating on a test tilts your life and the entire world to the side of Woe. You might want to read that last sentence again. And again. This is a heavy burden we carry.

By the same token, each act of Resistance—when you reel in your ego by admitting your jealousies to those you envy, or you give up your long-held, brilliant opinions for the sake of unifying with an opposing party, or you resist the urge to gain honor and prestige for yourself—tilts your existence, as well as all existence, toward the side of the Blessed.

The Opponent, as always, has ideas of his own. He will do his best to talk you out of this spiritual truth. He will try to make you reject this entire book by using your rational mind. He would rather sell you on ideas like "randomness" and "lucky and unlucky." Life is not that simple, he will tell you. We have no control, he will say. It is apparently better to overintellectualize, philosophize, and politicize all the events of our life and this world when seeking solutions.

But life is that simple.

"Simple" is not to be confused with "easy." These steps are challenging, and working them honestly and courageously will take you a lifetime.

The Zohar is a candle in a world of darkness. It transcends religion, race, gender, politics, and geography. All darkness, no matter how deep, gives way to the light of a single candle. And no amount of darkness can snuff out the Light.

Trying to live our lives with full accountability is perhaps the most difficult of all tasks. It is so much easier for us to take up causes, seek out new paths of wisdom, or try to change the world than it is to just look inward and try to change ourselves. But it helps to know that we are coming to the aid of the entire world when we do so. No longer are we to consider ourselves victims. From this point onward, we must accept responsibility for the rotten stuff that happens in our lives. We must admit that we are the cause. And being the cause is a good thing. It is one of the main attributes of being proactive, and one of the aspects the Vessel most sought. Only by being the cause can we begin not only to help ourselves but to help others as well.

This is quite a journey you have embarked upon. The more of the Light you receive, the farther you will be able to venture. You may want to read this book more than once. If you do, start a fresh journal, and work through the exercises anew each time. Everything is in constant change. So each day, start wherever you are. Shake yourself free of any expectation of arriving. Encourage yourself to be fully in the moment—to enjoy your transformations and to seek out new obstacles. Sink your teeth into the endless dessert, and make sure your neighbor has a nice juicy slice as well.

In an old kabbalistic tale, a student approaches his revered teacher and master and asks him to teach him all the sublime secrets and magnificent mysteries of the cosmos in the short time that it takes to remain balanced on one leg. Upon hearing his eager student's request, the eminent sage considers the question very carefully. His eyes then sparkle with infinite wisdom, and he says, "Love they neighbor as thyself. All the rest is mere commentary. Now go and learn."

○ We usually share character traits with the person who is driving us most crazy.

○ Judgment is a reactive behavior. It has nothing to do with transformation. We want to gently observe our character traits, not beat ourselves up about them.

○ You cannot change another human being. Think how hard it is to change yourself! And even if you could, you would only bring them Bread of Shame. They must make the change themselves.

○ We can, however, provide help on physical, mental, emotional, or spiritual levels, and we can attempt to influence others in ways we think would benefit them—or we can try to act in a manner and make decisions that would serve as a positive role model.

○ Teach, don't preach. To teach means to share your wisdom with others out of love and care, not because you want to convert someone. Or convince someone. Or sell to someone.

○ The Zohar describes this era as that of Woe and Blessed. We have a choice as to which way we experience it.

○ Remember, everything is inter-connected. Yelling at a friend or helping your kid sister with her math project both influence the complexion of the entire world.

○ All the wisdom in this book is contained in the adage "Love thy neighbor as thyself."

This one is fun. Sit down and make a long list of all the traits in others you find annoying, inappropriate, or downright wrong! Go into detail. Describe specific situations or encounters. How did this person look, and how did their voice sound? What in particular about these actions drove you nuts? Don't hold back. Make note of how you felt to be on the receiving end of these actions. Okay, now consider how many of these traits you may actually have yourself! What steps can you take to correct, or transform, them?

Q & A's

?&!

Q: **All of the girls at my school are skinny and they make fun of my extra weight. My parents say I'm beautiful just the way I am, but I don't feel beautiful. I know one of the girls started skipping meals and taking handfuls of diet pills and laxatives. Another eats gigantic meals, but throws them up afterwards. I want to fit in, but what should I do?**

A: According to Kabbalah, everything in our life that causes us pain, whether it's emotional or physical, occurs for one reason: To give us an opportunity to change a part of ourselves. Remember, if you react, by wanting to fit in and wanting to be skinny because your friends make fun of you,you have missed a wonderful opportunity to change yourself.

Your parents are profoundly correct in their answer. True beauty is the beauty of the soul. When you can resist reacting to the pressures of your friends and come to grips with the truth that you are indeed beautiful, then, according to Kabbalah, you will see miracles occur around you. Your friends will change. They too will see you for who you truly are. Or new friends who can offer you unconditional love and friendship will appear in your life. But it's up to you. If you continue to react to and fret over other peoples' reaction to your physical weight, nothing will change. When you resist those impulses and make an effort to find your true inner beauty, then the miracles will occur.

Q: **I think some of my friends would benefit from learning about Kabbalah. What is the best way to approach them on this topic?**

A: First, allow them to see the changes that are occurring within you. Being a living example and model of Kabbalah's wisdom is the most effective way to introduce people to this powerful teaching. Second, feel free to share some of the ideas that have touched you the most. But always remember, sharing is about teaching, not preaching. And teaching means being respectful and tolerant of where the other person is coming from. Make sure you are not trying to change your friends. Rather, you are sharing this wisdom with them in order to bring more Light and energy to yourself. If this idea is in your mind at all times, then you will be surprised how open your friends will be. Also, if by chance someone is not open, do NOT take it personally. Remember, you are sharing to bring more happiness to yourself, not to transform another person.

Q: **My best friend was just accepted into my number one college of choice. I haven't heard back yet regarding my standing. I am happy for him, but also jealous. What if I don't get in?**

A: It's wonderful and very powerful that you can admit that you are jealous. In order to find happiness in life, we must FIRST identify the negative traits that we have in our own character. Each negative trait is like a curtain that blocks out the Light. And remember, those curtains are a manifestation of our egos. As we remove more and more curtains (by identifying and admitting our nasty qualities), more Light will shine in our life. And that means we begin to receive everything we truly need. But keep in mind, in Kabbalah, we receive what we need,not necessarily what we want. Receiving what we need helps us to grow and become more fulfilled. In the end, that is all that really matters. If you do not get into the college of your choice, trust the Light and know that a better opportunity is coming your way. It will, if you retain that consciousness. If you worry and allow jealousy and frustration to fill your heart, then those negative feelings will become like self-fulfilling prophecies. The future will embody those self-destructive feelings.

Q **A lot of times at parties, kids are drinking or doing drugs. I don't need those to have a good time, but I'm afraid if I say no they will think I'm a loser.**

A Your classmates' desire to connect with higher realms of happiness and even spirituality can be a good thing, but unfortunately some kids confuse getting "high" from drugs or alcohol with getting high from a spiritual path. Although these substances may elevate a person into a higher state of consciousness, that sort of "high" never lasts. First off, you touch the Light directly, which we know causes a short-circuit and the inevitable crash. Secondly, the drugs and alcohol become the cause of your transcendence leaving you to be merely the effect. You are reactive instead of proactive. And remember, we came to this world to become the cause of our fulfillment; to do so we must be proactive. In addition to this, drugs have many negative side effects: addiction, poor health, poor judgment, not to mention depression and other forms of emotional pain.

If you let drugs and alcohol get you high then you are relinquishing control over your own life. Something external is affecting your happiness and generating a false feeling of well being. Thus, if you resist the short-cut that drugs offer, and instead focus on transforming your nature, then you will elevate to a high that lasts forever. Character transformation—identifying all your negative reactive traits and transforming them into positive proactive attributes--will deliver a greater high than drugs.

Therefore, if you feel pressure from your friends, RESIST the insecurity and anxiety that you feel. Stop worrying what they will think about you. The world is a mirror. If you are secure and rock solid in your desire to resist drugs for the purpose of connecting to the Light safely, your friends will sense that and respect you. If you are doubtful and concerned with their perception of you, they will mirror this behavior back to you and put increasing pressure upon you. Keep in mind that if people attach conditions to their friendship with you, such as partying with them, then they are not your true friends. Unconditional friendship means people accept you and love you with no strings attached. Thus, if you lose them, you never had them to begin with. When you begin to live life with this kind of mindset, and you continue to use Kabbalah's tools of resistance towards character transformation, the Light will bring you true friends who embrace you unconditionally.

Q: **My parents have been fighting all the time and recently they told me they are getting a divorce. I am angry at both of them for messing up my life, but I am also very sad. Will these steps will help me understand why they are doing this to me and how I can help?**

A: First off, it's natural to have many complex emotions around any change in our lives. And, yes, these 13 steps will help you very much as you sort this through. Remember to focus on being proactive rather than reactive. For instance, do not react to your parents fighting. Do not take it personally. It's not about you. It's about them. This will help create some space in which you can focus on the positive opportunities being presented to you.

As for the anger, see if you can't let that go. It might surprise you to learn that people come together in a marriage for the purpose of bringing a certain soul into this world. Once this is achieved, they often split up and move onto new partners who can help them in their own spiritual growth. Thus, in Kabbalah, divorce can also be a blessing! If two people are married, but they are not soul mates, they often divorce when they have earned the right to meet their true soul mate. Also any marriage that ends up in divorce is never considered a marriage that was wasted. Two people may have past life problems that they have to correct with one another. Once they make the correction, they divorce and find their next mate to help them correct and transform.

In Chapter Ten we discussed the belief that the greater the obstacle, the greater the potential Light. Hence, we welcome obstacles into our lives because they allow us to access the Light indirectly. This is how we grow and change. Your parents' divorce may in fact be the greatest obstacle you have faced thus far in your life. Kabbalah teaches that children choose their parents when they are still unborn souls in the Upper World. Thus, before you came to this world, you chose your parents because you foresaw all the obstacles and problems that would emerge from this family unit. Why would you choose such a situation? Simple. Because you saw that it would provide you with a wealth of opportunities to transform various character traits in your nature. Of course, when we enter the physical world, all this knowledge is lost and forgotten. Kabbalah helps us remember what we came here to do.

My boyfriend wants to have sex with me. I like him a lot but I'm scared. Plus, even though a lot of my friends are having sex now, I'd like to wait until I'm older. When I tell him this he seems to understand, but the next time I see him he tries all over again. How can I make this clear to him without losing him as my boyfriend?

If your boyfriend really loves you, he will respect your desires. If he keeps on trying then he is acting out of selfishness for his own desire and totally disregarding your feelings. That is not the basis for a healthy and loving relationship. There is a difference between love and need. Need means, "I want something from this person. They make me feel good. They give me pleasure." This is not sharing. This is receiving selfishly. True love means we care not only about receiving, but also giving and sharing. Never settle for less.

Q: A lot of my friends are having sex with girls but my girlfriend won't have sex with me. A bunch of kids at school know this and make fun of me because of it. I feel like I'm doing something wrong, but I don't know what. I really like her, but should I break up with her?

A: Why would you give up someone you care so deeply about, someone that treats you with respect and decency? Don't let peer pressure make you think that kindness isn't cool. The peers applying the pressure are usually doing so out of fear (i.e. fear that what they are doing is "wrong" therefore they get others to do it with them) and fear is one of the things we are seeking to transform through Kabbalah.

Q: Sometimes I get really depressed so that nothing matters to me anymore. Not my family, not my cats, not the paper I was working on for school. In those moments I want to die. In fact, I thought about committing suicide once or twice. What should I do?

A: Go out and share. Help someone who is in a worse situation than you. Find someone who is hurting more than you. When you share, you draw Light into your soul. And Light removes all the darkness and depression that we feel. Depression is merely a lack of Light. If you walk into a dark room you don't complain and worry about all the darkness. You simply flip on a light switch and the darkness vanishes. Sharing with people is our light switch. YES, IT IS THAT SIMPLE!

However, if your symptoms become worse, don't be afraid to seek out help. Allowing yourself to receive support from others can be as important as giving it to those in need. Contact the Kabbalah Teens Network at **1-877-K2TEENS** where our finest teachers are available to help you with these specific issues.

Q: **Most of the kids at my school come from families with a lot of money. They drive fancy cars, wear designer clothing and bring gourmet lunches. My parents can't afford any of this, but I often feel like I am less than my classmates simply because my parents don't make as much money. How should I handle this?**

A: Kabbalah teaches that before we come into this world, an unborn soul is shown his entire life in advance. Thus, we know ahead of time what difficulties we will encounter. We choose our parents and our circumstances because we know what part of our nature needs to be corrected. Your feelings of inadequacy may be part of your *Tikune*—karma or spiritual lesson. It is great that you have identified it as you now have something tactile to work with.

In addition, it sounds as though you are overly concerned with what people think about you. This is not unusual, especially with someone your age. Consider what it is you truly value in life. Instead of evaluating and judging people by the money they have, practice evaluating people by the goodness in their heart and their ability to offer friendship unconditionally. Over time, I think you will no longer notice if they pull up to school in a BMW or walk two miles in hand-me-down hiking boots.

Q: **I know that my parents love me, but the older I get the more they tell me all the things I'm not allowed to do, such as borrow the car or hang out with certain friends. Sometimes I get so angry I want to smash things, even things of mine that I really like. Is there something I can do to control this anger?**

A: There is only one reason why you should control your anger. Because controlling it will get you more Light in your life. Why? Because anger is a reaction. And reactions disconnect us from the 99%. When we resist anger WITH THIS KNOWLEDGE IN MIND, than we connect our souls to the 99% and we receive tremendous amounts of energy and Light in our life.

Q: **My friend's uncle raped me when I was 13. He told me not to tell anyone so I haven't. But I still have trouble sleeping at night. And I don't like to be alone in rooms with a guy. Is it my fault that he raped me? Is it all right to tell my parents or will they punish me?**

A: First of all, you should know that you did nothing wrong. It is absolutely not your fault that you were raped. Second, and I realize this may be difficult to absorb given the circumstances, every painful experience in our lives can be transformed into its exact opposite. In other words, all of your suffering, all your fears, all your hurt can be transformed into blessings and fulfillment. But you need to let go of the guilt and negative emotions you are carrying with you. This is not an easy thing to do. But every thing that happens in our life is there to teach us something about growing as a person. Everything. If you shift your thinking and your behavior into a sharing mode—by channeling your pain to help others—you will draw tremendous spiritual Light into your life. If you dwell on your own pain, even if justified, you will sink lower into depression and fear. Sharing with those who are in a similar or worse situation than our own is how we rise out of our pain. One of the first steps toward doing this is to talk to your parents about what happened to you. Don't suppress your feelings. Once all your fears and emotions are out in the open then, and only then, can you transform them into positive feelings.

As far as guys go, by focusing on sharing, on letting out and letting go of your negative emotions, you will create a situation where there is no fear and your true soul mate can find you. This is the power of the Light. When we connect to it, good things happen. The right things happen. Remember, the darkness in a room vanishes the moment a light bulb is turned on. The moment you connect to the Light, your darkness will vanish just as quickly.

Q: **My parents made me take advanced math so that I could get into a good college, but I don't understand most of the class! One of the students got a hold of the midterm and we're all supposed to meet up over the weekend to study it. In my mind I want to go so I can get an A in the class that will look good on my college applications. I bet my parents won't even care how I got the A, so long as I got it. But in my gut I think it's wrong to go. Please advise.**

A: Your gut is telling you to prioritize your own personal report card—recorded on your soul—over the fleetingness of a grade recorded on a piece of paper! This is not to say college is not important. Of course it is! But *how* you arrive at your "good college" is of more importance. Every time we think we can cheat and get away with it, we wind up paying for it. It may take 10 minutes. 10 months. Or 10 years. But make no mistake, the Law of Cause and Effect controls everything.

As we discussed in Chapter Seven, every negative seed we plant will cause a negative fruit to grow sometime in the future. Every positive seed we plant will eventually produce a positive fruit. The only thing that tricks us is "time." Because of time, the rewards of positive behavior can be delayed. This delay causes us to become doubtful about positive behavior. Because of "time" the negative consequences due to us as a result of negative behavior may also be delayed. This delay makes us think that we got away with our wrongful behavior. It's a trap. But it's a devious trap because negative behavior usually delivers a short-term reward and long-term payback in the future. The temptation to grab for the short-term reward is often very power-ful. But if you resist that desire, you will guarantee yourself Light and positive energy at some point in the future, and that will ben-efit you for the rest of your life.

The purpose of this book is to help you move through your teens with greater insight, compassion, love, abundance and intention. In support of this, The Kabbalah Center has established The Kabbalah Teens Network especially for you! It is a crisis, resource and referral hotline staffed by The Kabbalah Center's finest teachers. If you are struggling with depression, anxiety, suicide, troubles at home, at school, with friends, call us. It's free and it's confidential. Our counselors are trained to listen to your problems and help you find positive solutions. Or if you want to expand your Kabbalah education, call us! You can receive answers directly from a practicing Kabbalist, find out more about teen Kabbalah study groups in your area or get involved with local, national or international Kabbalah volunteer projects. Call **1-877-K2TEENS** anytime. Your path awaits you!

The Red String Book: The Power of Protection
By Yehuda Berg

Read the book that everyone is *wearing!*

Discover the ancient technology that empowers and fuels the hugely popular Red String, the most widely recognized tool of kabbalistic wisdom. Yehuda Berg, author of the international best-seller *The 72 Names of God: Technology for the Soul*, continues to reveal the secrets of the world's oldest and most powerful wisdom with his new book, *The Red String Book: The Power of Protection*. Discover the antidote to the negative effects of the dreaded "Evil Eye" in this second book of the Technology for the Soul series.

Find out the real power behind the Red String and why millions of people won't leave home without it.

It's all here. Everything you wanted to know about the Red String but were afraid to ask!

The Dreams Book: Finding Your Way in the Dark
By Yehuda Berg

In *The Dreams Book*, the debut installment of the Technology for the Soul Series, national best-selling author Yehuda Berg lifts the curtain of reality to reveal secrets of dream interpretation that have remained hidden for centuries.

Readers will discover a millennia-old system for understanding dreams and will learn powerful techniques to help them find soul mates, discover career opportunities, be alerted to potential illness in the body, improve relationships with others, develop an overall deeper awareness, and much more.

The dream state is a mysterious and fascinating realm in which the rules of reality do not apply. This book is the key to navigating the dreamscape, where the answers to all of life's questions await.

The 72 Names of God: Technology for the Soul™
By Yehuda Berg

The story of Moses and the Red Sea is well known to almost everyone; it's even been an Academy Award–winning film. What is not known, according to the internationally prominent author Yehuda Berg, is that a state-of-the-art technology is encoded and concealed within that biblical story. This technology is called the 72 Names of God, and it is the key—your key—to ridding yourself of depression, stress, creative stagnation, anger, illness, and other physical and emotional problems. In fact, the 72 Names of God is the oldest, most powerful tool known to mankind—far more powerful than any 21st century high-tech know-how when it comes to eliminating the garbage in your life so that you can wake up and enjoy life each day. Indeed, the 72 Names of God is the ultimate pill for anything and everything that ails you because it strikes at the DNA level of your soul.

The power of the 72 Names of God operates strictly on a soul level, not a physical one. It's about spirituality, not religiosity. Rather than being limited by the differences that divide people, the wisdom of the Names transcends humanity's age-old quarrels and belief systems to deal with the one common bond that unifies all people and nations: the human soul.

God Does Not Create Miracles. You Do!
By Yehuda Berg

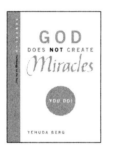

Stop "waiting for a miracle" . . . and start making miracles happen!

If you think miracles are one-in-a-million "acts of God," this book will open your eyes and revolutionize your life, starting today! In *God Does Not Create Miracles*, Yehuda Berg gives you the tools to break free of whatever is standing between you and the complete happiness and fulfillment that is your real destiny.

You'll learn why entering the realm of miracles isn't a matter of waiting for a supernatural force to intervene on your behalf. It's about taking action *now*—using the powerful, practical tools of Kabbalah that Yehuda Berg has brought to the world in his international best sellers *The Power of Kabbalah* and *The 72 Names of God*. Now Yehuda reveals the most astonishing secret of all:

the actual formula for creating a connection with the true source of miracles that lies only within yourself.

Discover the Technology for the Soul that really makes miracles happen—and unleash that power to create exactly the life you want and deserve!

The Monster Is Real: How to Face Your Fears and Eliminate Them Forever
By Yehuda Berg

What are you afraid of?

Just admit it! At this very moment, there's something (or maybe lots of things) that you're afraid of. No matter how convincing your fears may seem, this book will show you how to attack and defeat them at their most basic source. In *The Monster Is Real: How to Face Your Fears and Eliminate Them Forever*, Yehuda Berg, author of the international best-seller *The 72 Names of God*, reveals powerful, practical Kabbalistic tools for eliminating fear's inner causes once and for all. If fear in any form is bringing pain into your life, get ready for a hugely positive change. With *The Monster is Real*, another in the Technology for the Soul series, you'll learn how to conquer this age-old problem forever!

Health, happiness, and prosperity for:

Gideon Ben Chacham Oor
Pouran Bat Iran
Chacham Ben Gidon
Abraham Ben Gidon
Sharonah Bat Lida

9/05